THE WORSHIPFUL COMPANY OF BLACKSMITHS

Wrought-iron ink stand with oak leaf, mistletoe and flower decoration and the Company's Arms set with two brass ink pots and a bronze centre piece depicting two blacksmiths at work. Manufactured at J.E. Clarke's works in Featherstone Street, London, in 1890, it was presented by Prime Warden Thomas Poulter to commemorate the Company's First Exhibition of hammered iron work.

ALL OF THE PHOTOGRAPHS OF THE COMPANY'S TREASURES WERE TAKEN BY MICHAEL O'SULLIVAN

The Worshipful Company of Blacksmiths

David Hey

CARNEGIE

The author would like to thank the Wardens and the Clerk of the Company for their help, particularly with the final chapter of the book.

The Worshipful Company of Blacksmiths: A History

Copyright © Professor David Hey, 2010

First published in 2010 by
Carnegie Publishing *in association with* the Worshipful Company of Blacksmiths

Carnegie Publishing Ltd
Chatsworth Road,
Lancaster LA1 4SL
www.carnegiepublishing.com

All rights reserved
Unauthorised duplication contravenes existing laws

British Library Cataloguing-in-Publication data
A catalogue record for this book is available from the British Library

ISBN 978-1-85936-204-4   *hardback*

Designed, typeset and originated by Carnegie Publishing
Printed and bound in the UK by Henry Ling Ltd, Dorchester

Contents

Foreword *by* Alderman Sir David William Brewer CMG	vii
Introduction	1

1 The Medieval Guild and Fraternity — 3
Origins	3
Ordinances	8
The Medieval Blacksmith	14
The Fraternity of St Loy	16
Liverymen and Yeomen	19
The Blacksmiths' Hall	20

2 The Chartered Company — 27
Dissolution of the Fraternity	29
The Hall and Other Properties	30
The Royal Charter of 1571	32
Puritan Influence	39
The Royal Charter of 1639	41
Apprentices	44
Renovating the Hall	48

3 The New Blacksmiths' Hall — 51
Plague and Fire	51
Rebuilding the Hall	54
Royal Demands	59
The Blacksmith's Trade	60
Declining Powers	63
Apprentices	65

	Disputes and Challenges	67
	The Final Years of the Old Company	69
4	Finding a New Role	76
	The Rise of the Iron Industry	76
	The Traditional Blacksmith	77
	The Company	80
	Company properties	82
	Proposals for Reform	85
	New Initiatives	88
	Company business	91
	Wider Contacts	93
	County Shows and the Rural Industries Bureau	98
	Properties and business	102
5	The Modern Company of Blacksmiths	104
	The Livery	104
	Sponsorship of the Craft	107

Appendices

I	Events attended by the Prime Warden of the Worshipful Company of Blacksmiths, Keith Gabriel, 2008–09	118
II	The Masters, First, Upper or Prime Wardens of the Worshipful Company of Blacksmiths	123
III	The Blacksmith's Song	129
	Bibliography	131
	Index	132

Foreword

by ALDERMAN SIR DAVID WILLIAM BREWER CMG

Alderman Sir David William Brewer CMG, Prime Warden of the Worshipful Company of Blacksmiths, 2009–10.

As we approach the end of the first decade of the twenty-first century the City of London has maintained its position as the pre-eminent international financial centre. This is despite the economic vicissitudes, both domestic and international, that have been faced.

This strength has not been gained over a few years but over centuries and can be traced through the history of the Livery Companies and the entrepreneurs of the City, from the eighteenth century nascent financial markets as like-minded gentlemen gathered in City coffee houses, back to the Livery Companies and the early Guilds representing the mercantile, financial, market and craft interests of their members.

The City of London was vital to many monarchs and this is reflected in the unique rights conferred upon the Mayoralty, Shrievalty and Liverymen of the City. I was honoured to be Lord Mayor in 2005–06 and promoted the financial strength, abilities and innovation of the City throughout the world.

While that was most interesting, I particularly enjoyed the opportunity in the City to meet the Masters, Prime Wardens, Upper Bailiff, their Wardens and Liverymen, to see how Livery Companies, ancient and newly formed, act so dynamically now while drawing upon the centuries of tradition of the Livery movement.

Often this can be mildly amusing; such as the resolution of the 'sixes and sevens' debate about precedence between the Merchant Taylors' Company (my mother Company) and the Skinners' Company, but most often through the disciplines and responsibilities of centuries old traditions embodied in Charters and Ordinances that should still define business today.

When somebody is invited to become a Freeman of The Worshipful Company of Blacksmiths the Prime Warden says:

> *It is my duty to tell you that our Company is governed by laws*
> *embodied in Charters granted to us by past Sovereigns*
> *and is sustained by traditions and ideals handed down to us*
> *through many hundreds of years.*
> *Are you prepared to take an Oath that you will obey these laws,*
> *honour these traditions and further these ideals?*

Reflecting the religious origins of so many Companies you are not asked to assent or agree but to commit on your immortal soul!

The combined histories of the Livery Companies are the weft and warp of the life of the City of London, and I am privileged and delighted to introduce this newly commissioned history of The Worshipful Company of Blacksmiths during my year as Prime Warden of the Company.

When he was Prime Warden, John McCuin wished to mark his year in office in a tangible way. He therefore sought the means to build upon the 1930s history by Arthur Adams and the 1960s collation and publication of so much Company information by Past Prime Warden, and Honorary Archivist, Peter Rayner.

For many years John had known David Hey, Emeritus Professor of Local and Family History at the University of Sheffield, and a highly respected author, and so he approached him. The Blacksmiths' Company is fortunate in having one of the most extensive and complete Livery Company archives at the Guildhall Library. David has mined these sources to great effect in compiling this history. He has even exploded one of the myths of our date of incorporation that seems to stem from an error made in the nineteenth century.

His assiduous research and historical perspective have produced this excellent volume that combines the development of the Guilds of the City, the history of the Company and its contemporary importance to the craft, into an eminently readable and instructive whole.

It will stand for many years as a source of reference both to Blacksmiths and the wider City. It shows how The Worshipful Company of Blacksmiths has over the centuries combined the best of the Livery movement and of the City of London. This mirrors the development of the City of London, its ancient offices and modern businesses.

On behalf of the Court, Liverymen and the City I thank John McCuin for his initiative and David Hey for his erudition and research in providing the Blacksmiths' Company with this fine work. It will make us all more aware of our great history and commitment to the ancient craft.

David Brewer
Prime Warden
January 2010

John Strype's edition of John Stow's, *Survey of the Cities of London and Westminster* (1720) includes this fine map of 'Queen Hith Ward and Vintry Ward'. The Blacksmiths' Hall that was built after the Great Fire on the site of the original Hall is marked number 1 near the top of the map, on Lambeth Hill, where the ward boundary loops around it. The *Green Dragon Inn* and St Mary Magdalene's churchyard are shown nearby. The pattern of streets and alleys is the same as that which preceded the Great Fire of 1666. Lambeth Hill was an extension of Trig Lane, which led down to Wood Wharf on the River Thames.

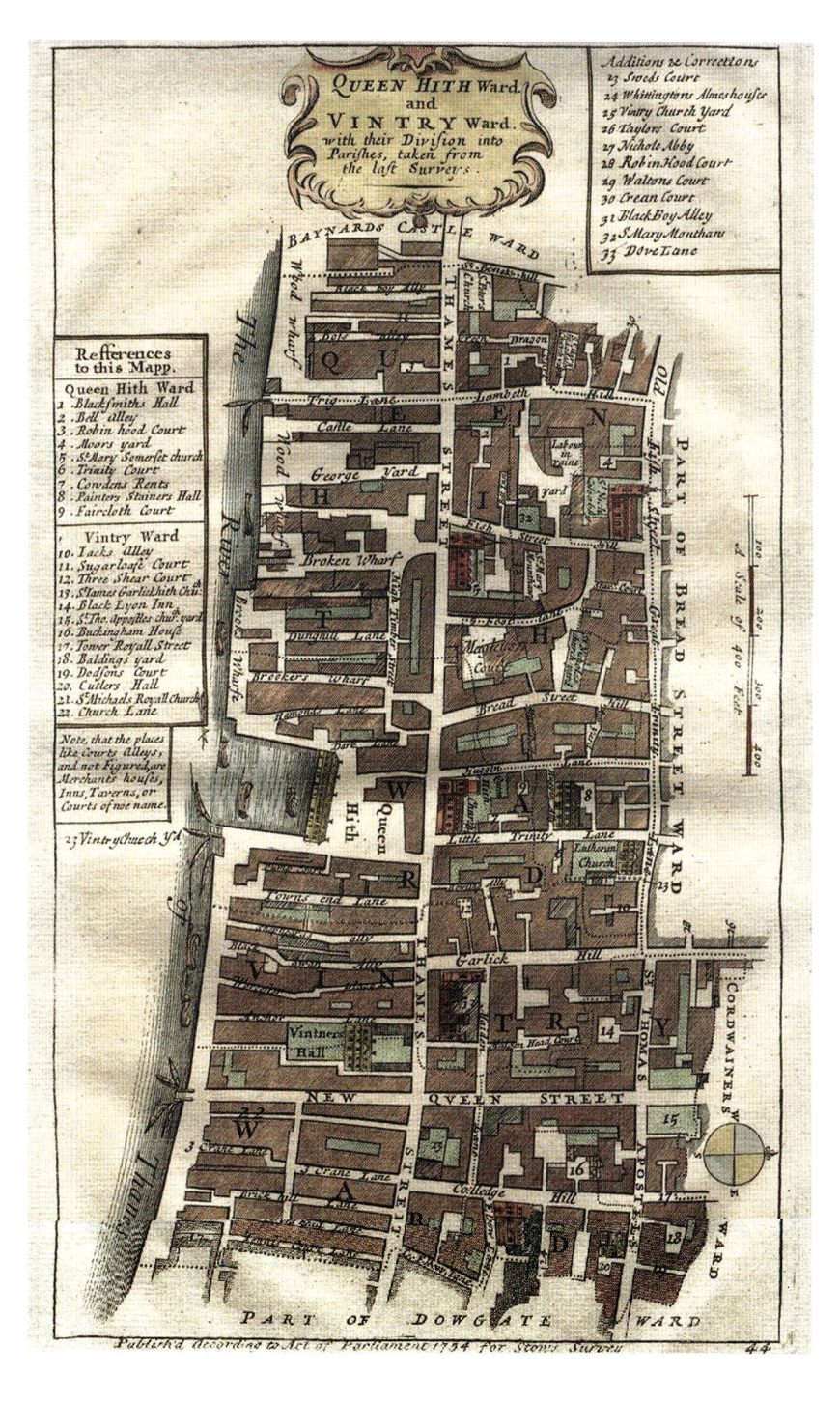

Introduction

The City of London has at present 108 livery companies. Some of these – such as the Worshipful Company of Security Professionals (2008) – are recent foundations, but most can trace their origins back well into the Middle Ages. They began as trade guilds for particular crafts, regulating such things as wages, hours of work and admittance to the trade, as well as guaranteeing the quality of products. They also acted as friendly societies, helping members who had become too old or ill to work and providing for their funerals. From the start, the livery companies were also associated with religious fraternities, which organised torch-lit processions to church services, and they provided social events, particularly annual banquets held in their livery halls. Together, they paraded on special occasions, such as when a monarch processed through London or at the installation of the Lord Mayor. They became a powerful economic, social and political force within the City walls and four miles beyond.

In 1515 the Court of Aldermen of the City of London settled an order of precedence on these grand parades, based upon the fortunes and influence of the 48 livery companies that were then in existence. The leading companies became known as the Great Twelve. The Worshipful Company of Blacksmiths was ranked 40th.

Medieval provincial cities, too, had their guilds and companies, some of which survive to this day, but these were far fewer in number than those in the populous and influential City of London. For centuries, London was not only the state capital, leading port, and most flourishing mercantile centre, but also England's greatest manufacturing city, with both highly skilled trades and relatively humble ones. Immigrants flocked into the City from all over England, and beyond, boosting London's population until it towered over the country's other urban centres. By 1700, London had a population of nearly half a million, whereas Norwich, the next largest city, had only 30,000 inhabitants.

Many of the London livery companies have shadowy beginnings as unauthorised groups of workmen seeking to regulate their trade. In time, they claimed prescriptive rights and eventually obtained royal charters. But the huge population growth eventually destroyed their powers, for they were unable to exert their authority when so many men set up as craftsmen without seeking membership. They survived as social organisations whose members were increasingly not connected with their particular trade, as valuable societies for networking among businessmen, and as charitable bodies that were often able to dispense large sums of money, particularly for educational and cultural purposes. Their purpose has changed, but they continue to play an important part in the ceremonial life of the City.

Most livery companies no longer have a strong connection with their original trade. Indeed, many of these trades have disappeared. The Worshipful Company of Blacksmiths, however, is fortunate in preserving its connections with a craft that is still basically the same as it was in the Middle Ages, though it is one that is now practised well outside the City's ancient boundaries. In recent decades the Company has made determined efforts to sponsor blacksmiths in many parts of Britain and to encourage some of them to become liverymen. In so doing, it has preserved its ancient traditions while continuing to encourage all that is best in the blacksmith's art.

The Medieval Guild and Fraternity

1

The history of the Worshipful Company of Blacksmiths goes back over seven hundred years. Like all ancient institutions, it has changed out of recognition over the centuries, but a thread of continuity is there. The evidence for the early years is patchy and often obscure, but enough survives for us to obtain a broad picture, sometimes enlivened with vivid detail.

Origins

The earliest document that provides information about the activities of an association of blacksmiths within the City of London is dated 7 March 1299. On that day sixteen men were brought before the 'City and Commonalty of London', that is the Mayor's Court, to answer the charge that they had formed an organisation, under oath, 'in contempt of the King and to the harm of the City'. This illegal organisation had been formed for mutual support and to prevent non-members from working at their trade. The organisers had sought to maintain or increase the prices of their products and to regulate their hours of work. They had drawn up a charter and the court was shown a box in which they kept their financial contributions. Their leader, John of Elsingham, admitted that the charter was in his custody and 'craved permission to bring it into court', but afterwards he said that he could not find it.

The other defendants admitted that they had unanimously made an ordinance to the effect that none of them should work at night, on account of the unhealthiness caused by coal fires and the disturbance of and possible damage to their neighbours, and that their doors should be closed all the year at the first stroke of the curfew bell at the parish church of St Martin's le Grand. This offers us a valuable clue as to where most of these early blacksmiths were living and working, for St Martin's le Grand is still the name of a street heading north from St Paul's Cathedral. However, as we shall see, John of

Wrought-iron mace with two applied enamel plaques depicting the Company's Arms, with a wood and wrought-iron stand.

Elsingham lived a mile or so further east in Cornhill Ward; the blacksmiths did not all live and work in one part of the City.

The defendants had also agreed that no members of their households should wander through the streets against the Proclamation (that is after the curfew had been rung to signal the end of the day) and that they had made the box so that each master of the trade of smiths could contribute a farthing a week to the maintenance of a wax taper to the honour of the Blessed Mary and St Loy, and also for the relief of any of the trade who should fall into poverty. St Loy was the patron saint of blacksmiths, and this reference to the religious aspect of their organisation explains why they were said to have 'impleaded persons who had offended them before the Ecclesiastical Court in lay pleas'. It seems therefore that they were well established before they were brought before the Mayor's Court in 1299, and that the Mayor and Aldermen were merely asserting authority over them. The jury that was called on 25 March 1299 brought in a verdict that 'the said John and the others were not guilty of the trespass, and that the said John did not have any charter in his custody contrary to the City'. The Court decided that 'the acknowledgments made were not prejudicial to the King or the Liberty', and so the defendants were acquitted. The blacksmiths had been reprimanded. They had learned to proceed more cautiously in future and to operate within the Mayor and Aldermen's jurisdiction.

An illustration from the *Holkham Bible* of c.1330, depicting the legend of the smith's ferocious wife forging nails for Christ's crucifixion, while her husband pleads that his injured hand prevents him for doing the job. The simple nature of the hearth, chimney, bellows, anvil, stock, and tools is revealed.

© THE BRITISH LIBRARY BOARD, MS ADD 47,682 F31

The leader of these sixteen smiths, John of Elsingham, probably came from the village of Elsenham, which lies between Bishop's Stortford and Thaxted in Essex, for the surname was recorded later as Elsynham. He was a man of some substance. In 1291 he was one of the two representatives of Cornhill Ward within the City of London who were named as 'the reputable men of each ward elected by common assent and consent of the whole Commonalty for the City's account'. In 1291 and in 1293 he was a witness to grants of property within Cornhill Ward to the Dean and Chapter of Canterbury Cathedral. He was probably well known to the Mayor and Aldermen when he was asked in their court to explain the nature of his blacksmiths' association, hence the leniency of their judgement.

The origins of most of the other fifteen men who were brought to court in 1299 are revealed by their by-names. Roger of Wodestrate was from Wood Street in the City of London and John and William of Sholane were from Shoe Lane just beyond the City wall in Faringdon, where the name was recorded as Scholane in 1283. Nicholas of Tottenham and Richard of Chigwell are straightforward names derived from well-known places not far beyond the City of London's borders. Lawrence and Michael of Wymbish came from the village of Wimbish, just to the east of Saffron Walden in Essex, and Andrew of Stibbenheth came from Stibben Heath, an old form of the place-name Stepney. Holt means a small wood and it is possible that John atte Holte and Stephen of Holte came from one of the places with that name in Epping Forest, but we cannot be sure. Two other men had migrated to the City from east coast ports: Robert of Sandwich from Kent and John of Goyppewyco from Ipswich. That leaves us with three men whose names were derived in a different manner: John May took his name from a pet form of Matthew, John the Simple's name came from an Old French word meaning 'honest, open, straightforward', and finally, Milo le Fevre, appropriately, had a Norman French name that meant 'smith'.

At about the same time that these sixteen men were challenged by the Mayor's Court, on 25 February 1299 a William of the Forest, smith, was brought there to answer the charge that for the past ten years he had traded with 'foreigners' (people beyond the jurisdiction of the City authorities) despite his not being a freeman. He claimed that he was a handicraftsman, not a merchant, and that he traded only with freemen. We do not know the result of this case, but on 7 April 1305 William appeared again before the Mayor's Court, this time defending the charge that he had beaten Adam of Clerkenwell, the beadle of Cornhill Ward, with a stick after the previous night's curfew. He was found guilty and his whetstone and two bellows were confiscated. The four men who were asked by the Mayor's Court to value this equipment in order to fine William were John of Elsingham, John atte Holte, John May, and Thomas of Wimbish, smiths, four of the sixteen men who had admitted membership of the fledgling Blacksmiths' Company six years earlier. They were clearly leading men in the trade, men who were respected by the Mayors' Court as responsible citizens.

The Spurriers, who eventually merged with the Blacksmiths, also found themselves in trouble with the Mayor's Court. On 7 January 1300 twelve named men 'and other spurriers' were summoned on a charge of 'having made an ordinance, confirmed by touching the Gospels, that no one of their trade of spurriers should do any work between sunset and sunrise'. Hugh Stroby had brought a suit before the Court claiming that his servant had been charged before the Archdeacon by these spurriers with having worked against the ordinance, 'and the said Richard, after being three times warned by the official, had been expelled from the church and excommunicated, until he would swear to keep the ordinance'. This action through an ecclesiastical court (because they were members of a religious fraternity) was now being challenged before the secular court that governed the City of London. Stroby also alleged that the spurriers had insisted that two makers of rowels (a sharp-toothed wheel inserted into the end of the shank of a spur) swear that they would not sell any of their products to him. He also claimed that the Spurriers' ordinances forbade anyone to take an apprentice for less than ten years and a premium of £2; that members of the fraternity would be defended at law if any case were brought against them; and that no member would work for or trade with anyone dwelling within or without the City who had not sworn to the ordinance. A jury was summoned, but before they met the parties had reached an agreement 'and the confederacy was condoned because nothing of it had yet been put into operation'.

It is clear from these cases in the Mayor's Court that by the end of the thirteenth century both the Blacksmiths and the Spurriers had formed organisations that developed into livery companies, though we cannot put a precise date on their foundations. In 1319 the king granted the Corporation of the City of London a charter confirming its ancient liberties; from then onwards no one was allowed to carry on his trade unless he was admitted to the Freedom of the City through his guild. There is no evidence to support the claim first made in the Blacksmiths' Company Court Minute for 5 January 1854 that the Company was incorporated by prescription by King Edward III in 1325, and as this king did not come to the throne until 1327 we should dismiss what was written over 500 years later as a misunderstanding. Like many of the London livery companies, the Blacksmiths did not go to the trouble and expense of obtaining a royal charter until several centuries later. They were content to function under the legal authority of the City from 1299 onwards.

Ordinances

The origins of most of London's medieval guilds are rarely as clear as in the cases of the Blacksmiths and the Spurriers. The Worshipful Company of Weavers is the first to appear in surviving records, when its charter dating from the first third of the twelfth century was confirmed in 1155. Fines levied in the Exchequer reveal the existence of guilds of Goldsmiths, Pepperers, Clothworkers, and Butchers by 1179–80; Loriners' ordinances (their bye-laws and regulations) survive from 1261 and Cordwainers' ordinances date from 1263; but by the end of the thirteenth century most guilds were still in their infancy. We first hear of the Carpenters in 1298, the year before the Blacksmiths, when they too formed an organisation to regulate working hours, apprenticeship, and the sale of goods. These early ordinances of the various London crafts that were submitted to the Mayor and Aldermen for approval were mostly rules that had been drawn up by masters to control their journeymen and apprentices. Journeymen were workers who had completed an apprenticeship but who had not become masters themselves; their name is derived from the French word, *journée*, for they were paid on a daily basis. Most of the City's craft guilds did not obtain full recognition from the Mayor and Aldermen, by submitting their ordinances for approval, until the fourteenth century. The history of the Blacksmiths' Company fits into this wider picture.

By about 1300 London's population had risen to between 80,000 and 100,000, a peak that would not be reached again until the reign of Queen Elizabeth I. This rapid rise resulted in overcrowding, shortage of work, intense competition, and poverty for many families. Craft associations aimed at protecting the interests of their members like an early trade union were a natural response to this hardship. Their members insisted that only freemen of the City should be allowed to practise their craft or trade and to sell their goods according to the rules and regulations laid down by the guild or company.

The articles and ordinances agreed by the Spurriers in 1345 pre-date the earliest surviving ones made by the Blacksmiths by a generation or so. As the Spurriers merged with the Blacksmiths towards the end of King Henry VIII's reign (between 1538 and 1546) it is worth examining these bye-laws. They start by enforcing the prohibition of work after the nightly curfew, rung from the parish church of St Sepulchre Without Newgate, on the grounds that 'no man can work so neatly by night as by day', and 'many persons of the said trade who compass how to practise deception in their work, desire to work by night rather than by day; and then they introduce false iron, and iron that has been cracked, for tin, and also, they put gilt on false copper, and cracked'. Worse still,

> many of the said trade are wandering about all day, without working at all at their trade; and then, when they have become drunk and enraged, they take to their work, to the annoyance of the sick and of all their neighbourhood, as well by reason of the broils that arise between them and the strange folks [i.e. those who were not spurriers] who are dwelling among them. And then they blow up their fires so vigorously, that their forges begin all at once to blaze; to the great peril of themselves and of all the neighbourhood around. And then, too, all the neighbours are much in dread of the sparks, which so vigorously issue forth in all directions from the mouths of the chimneys in their forges.

We can see why they needed regulating. In the future, anyone found working at night was to be fined 3s. 4d. for the first offence, 6s. 8d. the second time, and 10 shillings the third time; on each occasion 'one half thereof to go to the use of the Chamber of the Guildhall of London, and the other half to the use of the trade'. Anyone foolish enough to break the curfew a fourth time had to 'forswear the trade for ever'.

The other ordinances that were issued by the Spurriers at the same time were standard ones which insisted that only freemen of the City could pursue the trade, that apprentices had to be enrolled formally for at least seven years, that no master should take on another spurrier's apprentice, journeyman, or serving man who had entered an agreement, and that no one should work on Saturdays after noon had been rung out until the following Monday morning. On Sundays, spurs could be displayed at the front of a workshop, not for sale but purely to indicate the nature of the business.

Model of a blacksmith working at his anvil, made by Robert Hobbs and presented by Prime Warden Gordon A.P. Jewiss T ENG (CEI) in 1988. Robert Hobbs is a recipient of the Company's Gold Medal and a long serving member of the Craft and Awards Committees.

In 1368 six Blacksmiths were members of the Court of the Common Council of the City of London. The court had 148 members and no craft or 'mystery' had more than six. The term 'blacksmith' was only just coming into use; previously, they had been referred to simply as smiths. The first surviving articles or ordinances submitted by 'the reputable men of the trade of Blacksmiths' to the Mayor and Aldermen of the City are those of 1372. They start by ordering that:

> no one of the said trade shall cause any false work to be taken through the streets for sale in the City, or in the suburb thereof, or shall go

A detail of a map of London by Ogilby and Morgan, which dates from 1676, a decade after the City was devastated by the Great Fire. This section shows Cornhill running alongside the Royal Exchange near the top of the map, and 'Grace Church' or Gratious Street running north–south. 'St Benet Gracechirch' is marked at the cross-road with Lambart Street.

© THE BRITISH LIBRARY BOARD, MAPS, CRACE II, 61

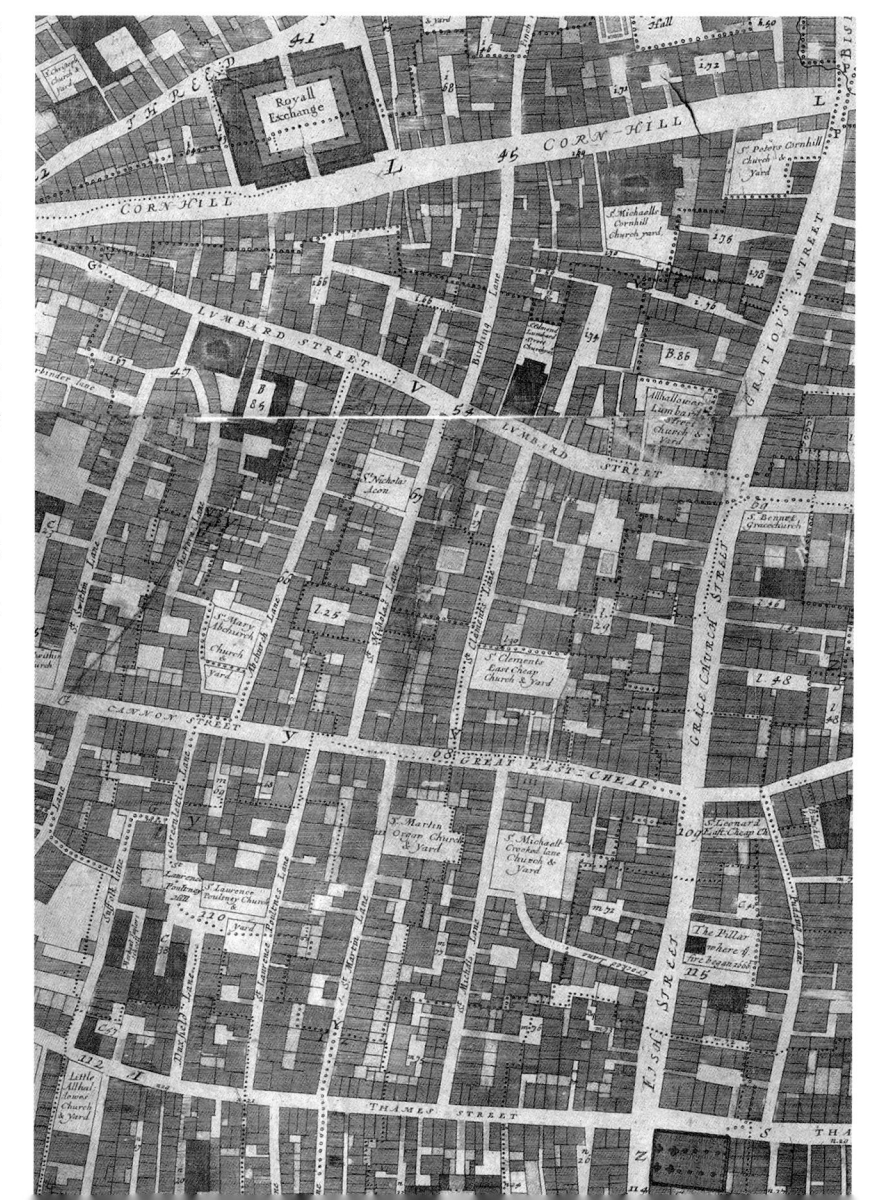

wandering about the said city, or the suburb, with such false work; but those who wish to send their work for sale out of their houses or shops, shall send the same to, and stand openly, at Graschirche, with such work for sale, or else upon the Pavement hard by St Nicholas Flesshameles, or near to the Tun upon Cornhulle.

Each of these places can be identified. The Tun in the wide street of Cornhill, where a corn market was held, was built in 1282 as a temporary prison for night offenders such as 'prowling thieves, street-walkers and other disreputable people' who had ignored the curfew bell. Its name came from its resemblance to a huge barrel of wine. St Nicholas Fleshambles was the church in Newgate, on the other side of St Paul's Cathedral to Cornhill, where butchers offered meat for sale from their stalls. 'What a shambles!' is still a phrase that we use for a disorderly mess, and the street where the butchers congregated in York is still known as The Shambles. 'Graschirche' is commemorated by the present Gracechurch Street, which forms a junction with Cornhill. In medieval times a grass or hay market was held near the church that became known as St Benet Gracechurch, where Fenchurch Street and Lombard Street cross Gracechurch Street. This church was rebuilt after the Great Fire, but was demolished in 1868. These, then, were the open-air markets where blacksmiths offered their wares for sale. Customers could, of course, buy directly from a blacksmith's shop in front of his house. Others products were sold to ironmongers who had much wider contacts and who travelled to provincial fairs. Yet, curiously, the medieval and early-modern records of the Blacksmiths' Company never mention the Company of Ironmongers, one of the 'Great Twelve' companies, which obtained a royal charter in 1463, nor any individual ironmongers.

The brief ordinances of 1372 contain other clauses that were standard ones for medieval guilds, with penalties for infringements. They insisted that 'every master in the said trade shall put his own mark upon his work, such as heads of lances, knives, and axes, and other large work; that people may know who made them'. The next clause ordered that any 'false work … made in the trade' (that is by non-freemen) should be taken to the Guildhall for judgement. No man was granted his freedom until the Master and Wardens of the Blacksmiths' Company judged his competence and accepted the quality of a 'proof piece' that he had submitted for their approval, and no one was allowed to take on another master's apprentices or journeymen.

The growth and activities of the numerous London guilds and fraternities was a matter of concern to the Crown and Parliament in the troubled years of the reign of King Richard II, culminating in the major uprising of 1381. This is known, somewhat misleadingly, as the Peasants' Revolt; in fact, the rebellion was as much urban as rural and the worst troubles occurred in London. On 17 October 1388 Parliament made 25 proposals to improve law and order in the City. They began by proposing that 'badges and liveries, such as distinctive hoods, should be abolished', as should 'all guilds, fraternities and their common chests'. They then suggested that livery company funds should be confiscated to cover the expenses of the war with France. The King did not agree to these proposals, but he pacified Parliament by instigating an enquiry into the activities of the City's guilds and religious fraternities. No firm decisions arose from this, but it did prompt many guilds to apply for a royal charter that would license them to wear a livery, hold property, and draw up their own rules. The Blacksmiths, however, had little or no property at that time, so like many of the poorer crafts they continued to follow the old method of seeking approval for their ordinances from the Mayor and Aldermen. During the later period 1460–1500 at least sixteen of the London craft guilds had their ordinances enrolled in the City's Letter Book, and in 1487 the Mayor and Aldermen demonstrated their authority by ordering that any ordinances that they had not approved had to be cancelled.

The concern for stricter regulation in the troubled years after the Peasants' Revolt led to the twice-yearly swearing in of the 'Masters of Misteries' at the Mayor's Court. (Medieval crafts were often referred to as mysteries, as in the performance in some cities, such as York or Coventry, at Corpus Christi of Mystery Plays.) In 1391 Walter West and John Kempe were sworn in for the Blacksmiths and Roger Godesfast and Adam Rande succeeded them the following year. It seems that, in those years, the Blacksmiths' Company were led by two Wardens only. New ordinances that were submitted by the Blacksmiths to the Mayor and Aldermen for approval in 1394 were more detailed than those of 1372. The Blacksmiths began by acknowledging, like the Spurriers before them, that the proximity of smiths' forges to other people's houses could be a fire risk and a nuisance. It seems likely that the Mayor and Aldermen had told them to address this problem. The clause follows a standard format and reads:

> In the first place, forasmuch as the folks of the said trade of Blacksmiths are often times indicted at divers Wardmotes, from Ward to Ward, and warned to quit their houses, by reason of the great nuisance,

noise and alarm experienced in divers ways by the neighbours around their dwellings; it is ordained that from henceforth no one of the said trade shall work by night, but only from the beginning of daylight to 9 of the clock at night throughout all the year, except between the Feast of All Hallows [1 November] and the Feast of Candlemas [2 February]; between which Feasts they shall work from 6 of the clock in the morning until 8 of the clock at night. And also, no one of the said trade shall work at all in his shop on any Saturday, or on the Eve of a Feast which is itself an Eve, after the first stroke of the bell rung for Vespers; on pain of paying, every one of the trade who shall be found in default, and culpable as to the said points, the first time 40*d.*, the second time 6*s.* 8*d.*, and the third time 13*s.* 4*d.* And so every time afterwards, when any default shall be found, the same penalty shall each time be paid; one half to go to the use of the Chamber of the Guildhall, and the other half to the use of the said trade.

The second clause confirms that the Blacksmiths' Company had just two Wardens in command and that they were elected at Michaelmas. No reference was made to a Master. The clause reads:

They shall be enabled to elect, and shall elect, every year, about the Feast of St Michael the Archangel [29 September] two able men of the said trade, to be their Wardens for the ensuing year, and shall present them to the Chamberlain of the Guildhall, to take their charge to govern and rule all those who constantly follow the said trade within the City, and the suburbs thereof, in their degree, the same as the Wardens of other trades in the same city do. And if the Wardens of the preceding year shall not present to the Chamberlain aforesaid within eight days after the Feast of Simon and Jude [28 October] the Wardens newly chosen for the ensuing year, then, for such default, the old Wardens shall incur the penalty of 20 shillings; to be levied, that is to say, one half to the use of the Chamber, and the other half to the use of the trade. And if any one so elected shall refuse such office and charge, such person shall incur a penalty of 20 shillings; one half to go to the Chamber and the other half to the use of the said trade.

The third clause allowed the Company to search for, and confiscate, inferior wares and for products made by those who were not freemen, within the City and its suburbs (which were customarily defined as being within four miles of the City walls). It reads:

> The Masters for the time being of the said trade shall make their search within the franchise of the City, and in the suburbs thereof, for all manner of work of their trade, for retail, in the hands of freemen of the trade; and shall bring in all false work, and not marked, as being forfeited, to the Guildhall, to be adjudged upon by the Mayor, or by the Chamberlain; and that such loss by forfeiture shall fall as well upon him who has made false work, as upon him who has made work, and has not put his mark thereon.

The fourth clause addressed a particular problem that had arisen concerning the dishonest manufacture of keys. It shows that the Company were determined to control the quality of products in order to preserve the good reputation of the craft. The ordinance reads:

> No manner of man following the said trade in the City, or in the suburb thereof, shall make any manner of key from any kind of impress thereof, unless he have the key itself present, or the lock to which the same key has to be made; by reason of the mischiefs which have happened, and which may happen in time to come. And whosoever shall be found from henceforth in default on this point, and shall be convicted thereof, he shall abide by the judgement and award of the mayor and Aldermen thereon.

Finally, it was agreed that:

> No man of the trade shall carry, or cause to be carried, any manner of work of the said trade to any fair, before the said work shall have been shown to the Wardens for the time being of the trade, as being good and lawful to serve the people, on the pain above specified.

The Medieval Blacksmith

Medieval illustrations show blacksmiths wearing long leather aprons as they worked at the forge, to protect themselves against sparks when they hammered a bar of red-hot iron held by tongs on an anvil set firmly in a thick trunk of wood. Strength was needed not just for the hammering but to blow the bellows to get a fierce fire burning in the hearth. The flames, smoke and noise coming from the forge, especially when work continued illegally into the night, was a common cause of complaint from neighbours. A poem written in the late fourteenth or early fifteenth century on an earlier manuscript at Norwich Cathedral Priory complained that swarthy smiths, smattered with smoke, drove the author to distraction by the din that they made in the night time. Their cries and clatter as they 'blow their bellows till their brains are bursting' and the clanging of their heavy hammers as the iron was struck on the anvil was more than he could bear. His antagonism may have run deeper than this, for the flames from the smith's forge were associated in the clerical mind with the fires of hell. This association is brought out by an illustration in the *Holkham Bible* of *c.*1330, which famously portrays a ferocious-looking smith's wife forging nails for Christ's crucifixion while the smith himself pleads that an injured hand disables him from doing the job. The popular early fourteenth-century poem, *The Northern Passion*, described the smith's wife in this legend as 'a fell woman and full of strife'.

It is surprising that women were involved at all in the heavy work of the smith. They are mentioned only fleetingly in the archives of the Blacksmiths' Company. Widows were allowed to manage their deceased husband's business, but sometimes women took a more active role. Crown records reveal that Katherine, the widow of the king's smith, Walter of Bury, had learned the trade from her husband. In 1346 she was paid 8*d.* per day to 'keep up the king's forge in the Tower and carry on the work of the forge' while her son, Andrew, was a soldier in France. In 1348 she appears in the royal records as the 'smith-wife' who worked at Westminster 'steeling and battering the masons' tools'.

Wrought iron, which had been produced on a small scale in water-powered furnaces since the fourteenth century, was brought up the Thames to the City's wharfs from the Weald of Kent and Sussex, and from many parts of the Continent. From about 1500 it became more common to cast iron into moulds in a blast furnace, but most output was refined at the forge and was sold to the secondary metalworkers as wrought-iron bars and rods. Steel had to be imported from the Continent and so was used only in small portions, especially when a sharp cutting edge was needed for tools and weapons.

The wide range of objects that were made from wrought iron included the various types of nails, hinges, staples, pins, and wedges that were used in the construction industry; bolts, screws, and locks and keys for chests and

A fourteenth-century illustration from the Netherlands, showing blacksmiths at work in their leather aprons. Immediately evident from this evocative image is the physical labour involved in hammering a red-hot bar of iron on an anvil standing on a wooden stock. The primitive hearth is blown by a pair of bellows. Few tools other than hammers and tongs were needed.

© The British Library Board, Sloane 3983, F.5

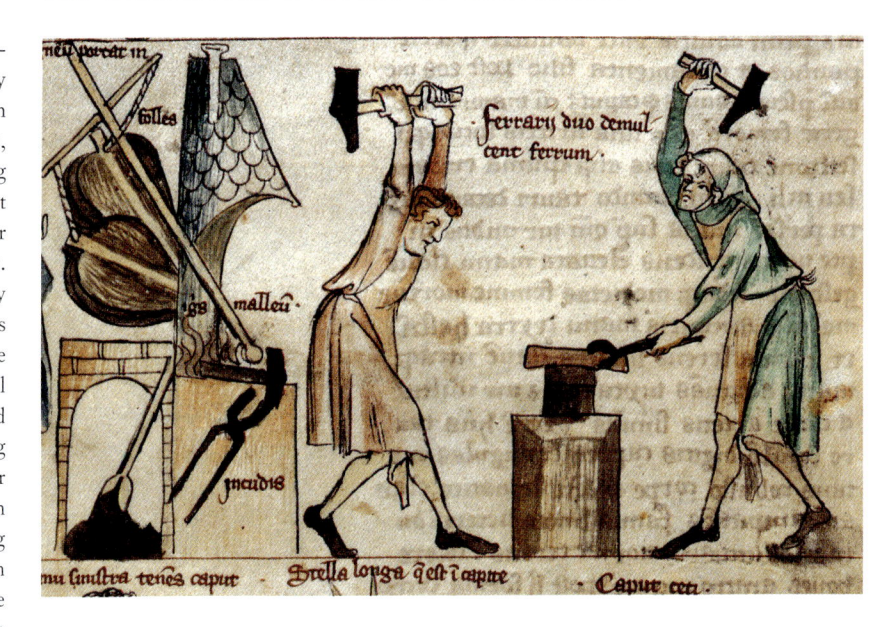

doors; grates, bars, pokers and other iron furniture for the hearth; pots, pans, kettles, and smoothing-irons for domestic use; axes, hatchets, chisels, files, tongs, pincers, hammers, vices, and the metal parts of woodworkers' tools; guns, pistols, daggers, swords, armour, anchors, and cannon for the army and navy; and clocks and decorative pieces such as the scrolls that adorned church doors. The blacksmith's trade overlapped with that of the bladesmith, spurrier, loriner, pinner, farrier, gunsmith, armourer, and clockmaker, and this of course often led to disputes. Drawing teeth (without an anaesthetic) remained a side-line for centuries, as it did for blacksmiths in the countryside.

The Fraternity of St Loy

Medieval craft associations were not just driven by the need to earn a living and the desire to agree regulations that all should abide by. From the start, they had religious and social dimensions as well. They were designed to provide mutual support during life in the form of convivial gatherings and charitable donations to poor members, and provision for death in the form of funerals attended by all members, regular prayers to assist the soul in its passage through purgatory, and commemorative masses. It was normal for a craft guild to be associated with a fraternity or religious association, dedicated to an appropriate saint. The patron saint of blacksmiths, and some other metalworkers, was St Eloy, or St Loy for short, a seventh-century goldsmith and preacher who became the bishop of Noyon, in northern France, in 641. His cult spread to England, where Chaucer's Prioress's strongest oath was 'by St Eloi!'. His principal emblem was a horseshoe and he was depicted holding the devil by the nose with a pair of pincers. His feast day, 1 December, was commemorated by the fraternity that was associated with the Blacksmith's Company. We have seen that, as early as 1299, the Blacksmiths maintained a wax taper in honour of St Mary and St Loy in a church that cannot now be identified. By the fifteenth century the City of London had over 200 religious fraternities, most of which were not associated with guilds but were focused on the parish church of a particular neighbourhood.

Among the records of the Blacksmiths' Company at the Guildhall are the ordinances, articles and constitutions ordained and granted by 'the Worshipful Master and Wardens of the brethren of St Eloy at the feast of Easter 1424 with the whole company of the Craft of Blacksmiths who assemble in the church of St Thomas of Acre and go thence to the Greyfriars in London'. Here we come across the terms Worshipful and Master for the first time, though they may have been in use earlier. The Hospital of St Thomas of Acre was the medieval London headquarters of the Knights of St Thomas, an order that had been established in the Holy Land at the time of the third crusade, when the cult of St Thomas Becket was spreading throughout Europe. The hospital stood at the corner of Old Jewry and Poultry, just off Cheapside, half way between Cornhill and St Martin's le Grand. It occupied the site of the house where Becket had been born, in the parish of St Mary Colechurch. Between the thirteenth and the sixteenth century many London citizens were buried in the hospital church and numerous civic ceremonies were held there, including those of various livery companies such as the Blacksmiths. The Worshipful Company of Mercers eventually built its hall on this site. From this church, the fraternity of St Loy paraded behind the bearers of wax torches and the carriers of banners adorned with the saint's image along Cheapside and Newgate to a service in the early fourteenth-century church of the Franciscan order, popularly known as the Greyfriars. This enormous Gothic church was the second-largest ecclesiastical building in medieval London; it measured 300 feet long by 89 feet broad and had at least eleven altars. It prospered through extensive royal patronage and the contributions of thousands of Londoners.

The membership of the fraternity of St Loy included not only blacksmiths, but farriers (who shoed horses) and loriners (who made bits, spurs and the metal parts of harness). The list of members in 1424 is difficult to read as it is rather cramped and the ink has faded, but there seem to have been about

Section of a large view of the City of London by Ralph Agas (died 1621), which is based on a much earlier one from before the Reformation. This detail shows the Greyfriars' church to the north of Old St Paul's Cathedral. Every year, the fraternity of St Loy walked in a torch-lit procession from St Martin's le Grand (*right*) past the fish shambles in Newgate to the friary church.

BY KIND PERMISSION OF THE GUILDHALL ART GALLERY, CITY OF LONDON

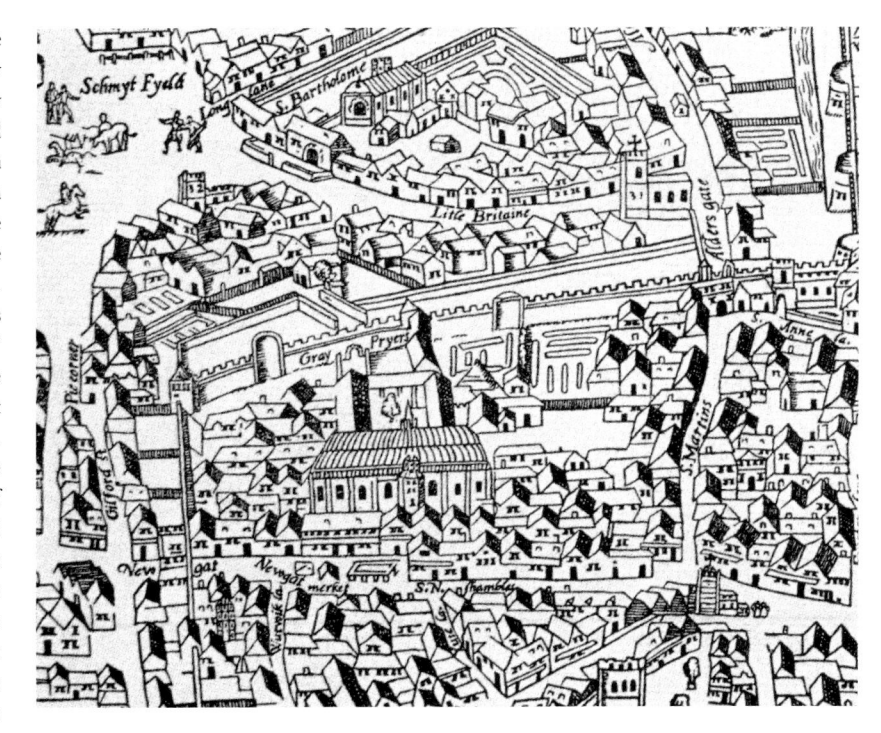

53 blacksmiths and their wives and 15 single blacksmiths, about 30 farriers and their wives and eight unmarried farriers, and 25 loriners and their wives and one unmarried loriner, a total of about 240 brethren and sisters of the fraternity, headed by William Johnson, blacksmith. Elections were held on the day of the Feast of St Loy, 1 December, and 'Coney Feasts' – so called because the fraternity dined on rabbits, considered a delicacy at that time – were held each Quarter Day, when subscriptions were due. On such formal occasions, members were expected to dress in the appropriate clothing, or livery. Meanwhile, the Spurriers' Company had its own fraternity of 'brethren and sisters' dedicated to St Katherine the Holy Virgin; the ordinances that they made in 1421 survive with the records of the Blacksmiths' Company at the Guildhall, for the two companies eventually merged.

The dual nature of the Blacksmiths' Company as a craft guild and religious fraternity is glimpsed in further 'ordinances, articles and constitutions' agreed in 1426. These name a Master ('Maister') as well as the two Wardens. These leaders were to be 'substantial and honest men of the same craft' chosen by 'common assent'. One of their duties was to look after 'the Common Box' to which every quarter of a year each man who wore the livery was expected to contribute 2*d*. and every sister of the fraternity 1*d*. These funds paid for the burials of members of the fraternity and were the source of charitable donations of 6*d.* a week to members who had fallen into poverty. In that way, the fraternity fulfilled a similar role to the friendly societies of later centuries. The ordinances also confirmed that the Company's feast was held on St Loy's day or the following Sunday, when every brother was expected to pay 12*d.* for his meal and every sister 8*d.* Finally, a dirige or mass for the souls of deceased members of the fraternity was held on the afternoon of St Andrew's day (30 November), the day before the annual feast. A dirige, or dirge, was so-called because that is the Latin word for 'Direct Thou', the first antiphon of Matins for the dead.

LIVERYMEN AND YEOMEN

These references to the wearing of a livery are the first that we have for the Blacksmiths, though the practice may already have been ancient by the 1420s. At a reception for King Edward I's second wife, Margaret, in 1300 all the citizens of London had worn a livery of red and white; the various crafts were distinguished only by the emblems that were displayed on their sleeves. The 1388–89 Crown enquiry found that by that time the common practice of the wealthier associations was to wear a special company livery or at least a common hood. The livery cloth was bought by the company and each member then paid for the piece that was tailored to fit him.

Each of the London livery companies was faced with the problem of what to do with the younger freemen who were starting up in the trade and the large numbers of journeymen who had completed an apprenticeship but who worked for wages. The answer was to provide an association for the rank-and-file within the larger body. These groups were known as Yeomanries. They should not be confused with the militia men, or yeomanry, of Victorian times. A yeoman was originally a knight's young servant or retainer, and this sense of the word was extended to include young workers of many different kinds. For instance, one of Chaucer's *Canterbury Tales* was told by the Canon's Yeoman.

The medieval records of the Court of Commissary of the Bishop of London contain ordinances of just four guilds. Fortunately, one of these was that of the fraternity of St Loy with 'the whole company of the craft of blacksmiths who assemble in St Thomas of Acre and thence to the Grey Friars'. At Easter 1434 they ordained that the procession to the Grey Friars church should be led by 'servants of the brotherhood' in front of 'the masters of the craft'. Absentees would be fined by 'the wardens of the brotherhood of yeomen' and each servant was expected to pay for a pound of wax for the torches. New members of the yeomanry had to pay a two shillings entry fine, then a yearly subscription of 2d. The ordinances go on to say that the 'beadle of the yeomen' was paid a salary out of quarterly subscriptions, with extra income from notifying members in person of company events and arranging funerals. Every two years at the Feast of St Loy the yeomen chose a new Master or Warden. A man who had been 'Warden of the Yeomen' could not be re-appointed within the next six years.

The Yeomanry within the Blacksmiths' Company was already well established by 1434. The ordinances note:

> a remembrance that in the time that William Ferour was Warden of Blacksmiths and Governor of Yeomen of the Blacksmiths in that time John Water, John Spencer, Jeffrey More, and John Lamborn, Masters of the Yeomen aforesaid and twelve of the same Company: we have ordered that every brother shall pay the first day 6d. and every wife of the said brethren 4d., and also at the quarter day every man and his wife 3d. If any of the said brethren or their wives be absent from our common dinner or from a quarter day shall pay as much as if present.

The members of this subordinate body within the Blacksmiths' fraternity were clearly journeymen or servants who worked for wages. Their financial rewards were meagre. The 1434 ordinances declared that qualified craftsmen coming into London had to serve two weeks without pay and then enter into a contract with a freeman at a salary of £2 a year. This compares with the £16 or so per annum that a master could earn. By the end of the fifteenth century most livery companies had a yeomanry. The character of these bodies changed over time, but in the Middle Ages they played a useful role in channelling the energies of the young and in ensuring that they remained under the discipline of the parent company.

The Blacksmiths' Hall

It was the ambition of every London livery company to possess its own hall. The granting of royal charters to the better-off companies stimulated the erection of large, timber-framed buildings where dinners could be held and the wealth and standing of the organisation displayed. It has been estimated that whereas perhaps only half a dozen halls had been erected or adapted in the City by 1400, their number had grown to 37 by 1500 and to 47 by 1540. The experience of the Blacksmiths' Company again fits this wider pattern.

Cornhill Ward and the district further west on the northern side of St Paul's Cathedral were of special importance to the Blacksmiths from the earliest days, but when the Company came to lease a hall from the Mayor and Corporation to act as a centre for their activities they chose a site that lay a little further south, between St Paul's and the Thames, on the boundary between Castle Baynard and Queenhithe Wards. Perhaps it was simply the nearest convenient site that was available? We have no clue as to why it was chosen, nor do we know when the hall was built. Our first evidence is a lease of 2 June 1494, but as the building was already well stocked at that time and was built in the typical style of a medieval hall, this lease might well have been a renewal. Equally, the hall might have been built for another purpose and

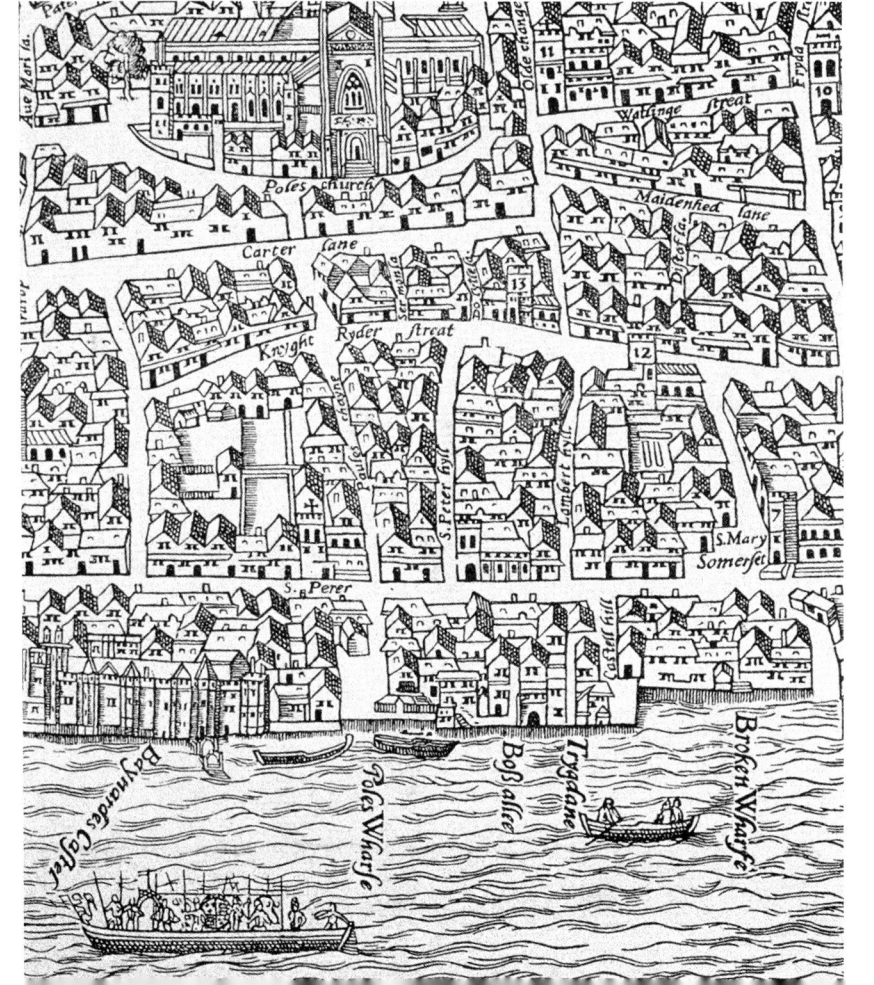

Detail of the 'Agas view', depicting the original Blacksmiths' Hall in the mid-sixteenth century. The Hall stood on Lambeth Hill, on the route from the River Thames up Trig Lane to St Paul's Cathedral.

BY KIND PERMISSION OF THE GUILDHALL ART GALLERY, CITY OF LONDON have come on the market at the right time for the Blacksmiths to take it over. The lease from the 'Mayor, Aldermen and Common Council' to the 'Wardens and Fellowship of Blacksmiths' was for 80 years at an annual rent of £3.

The site, 'beside Lamberth Hill in the parish of Mary Magdalene in Old Fish Street in the Ward of Queenhithe', can be identified from seventeenth- and eighteenth-century maps that show the second Hall, which succeeded the medieval one after the Great Fire of London in 1666. The Hall stood half way up Lambeth Hill, a continuation of Trig Lane coming from the Thames, and next to the Green Dragon Inn. Lambeth Hill was known originally as Lambart Hill and was recorded as such in 1283. In his *Survey of London*, first published in 1598, John Stow wrote, 'Last of all, have you Lambart hill lane, so called of one Lambart owner thereof; and this is the furthest west part of this warde' (Queenhithe Ward). He went on to mention 'the Blacke smithes Hall (which is about the middle of this lane)'. The parish church of St Mary Magdalene, which was just up the road by a fish market, was the natural choice for the Blacksmiths. It is likely that they had their own altar there, dedicated to St Loy. This church was destroyed in the Fire, rebuilt by Wren in 1685, severely damaged by fire again in 1886, and demolished in 1893. The site is now covered by post-War development and the old streets survive only in mutilated form. Confirmation that the original Blacksmiths' Hall was on the same site as the one built after the Fire is provided by a list of 'The Inhabitants of London in 1638', which noted that the parish of 'St Maudlin near Old Fish Street' contained the Blacksmiths' Hall, next to the Green Dragon, and 'Houses on Lambert Hill'.

As the hall was completely destroyed in the Great Fire and we have no detailed drawings of it, it cannot be dated by its style or by the modern technique of dendrochronology (a computerised form of tree-ring dating). However, we get a good impression of it from a detailed inventory of 'the goods belonging to the fraternity of St Loy of the craft of Blacksmiths of London within their hall' that was made on 3 December 1496, shortly after the fraternity's annual feast and not long after the taking of a lease of the site. It is clear from the inventory that the hall was built in the typical medieval style, timber-framed and open to the rafters in the centre of the building, with a parlour and a chamber above it at one end, and with the service rooms at the other end separated from the hall by a through passage with a screen below a minstrels' gallery. This arrangement is preserved in the medieval halls of some Oxford and Cambridge colleges, in manor houses such as Penshurst (Kent), Gainsborough Old Hall (Lincolnshire), or Haddon Hall (Derbyshire), and in the medieval guildhalls at York, though the Hall of the Blacksmiths' Company would have been on a smaller scale.

As was usual, the timber roof trusses were exposed to view and colour was provided by wall hangings. These included three borders of linen cloth stained black and red and depicting crowned hammers and roses, presumably Tudor roses to signify loyalty to the Crown, and banners of red buckram (a coarse linen or cotton fabric stiffened with paste), displaying the arms of the craft and supported by two shafts. The first grant of arms to the Blacksmiths' Company had been made by Sir Thomas Holme, Clarenceux King of Arms, only a few years earlier on 12 April 1490. The arms featured a phoenix with a crown of gold and a chain, three hammers crowned with gold, and the motto: 'As God will so be it'. They are illustrated in the margins of the Company's earliest charters. Equally striking were the three garlands sewn with purple velvet, suns of silver gilt, and the image of St Loy. The main body of the hall was decorated with a cloth above the high seat of the Master, 7¼ yards long and three yards broad, and with slightly smaller cloths on the east and west sides. The high seat was placed in the middle of a table that was thirteen feet long and a yard broad and which was supported by trestles on a slightly raised dais facing the gallery at the other side of the room; two forms, each six feet long, provided seating. Another long table, with trestles and forms, stretched along the west side of the hall. In the centre of the hall heating came from a fire which was contained within 'a round fire pan of copper bounded with iron', the gift of John Crocherd, the current Master; the smoke escaped through a louvre in the roof in the usual manner of medieval halls.

A more private room on the ground floor, known as the parlour, was used for meetings of the Master and Wardens and other small gatherings. It, too, had painted cloths hanging on the wall and an alabaster image of St Loy. Alabaster was quarried in the Trent Valley and was highly esteemed for carved monuments, especially effigies in churches, so the Company must have been reasonably prosperous to commission such a work. The furniture consisted of two tables and trestles, but no forms were mentioned. The room was heated by a fire pan and chimney. The chamber above the parlour – the only room at the upper level of the building – was furnished simply with a table, trestles and forms.

The minstrels' gallery above the screen at the opposite end of the hall was also adorned with a painted cloth and provided with a long table, trestles and forms. Beyond the passage that ran behind the screen were the pastry house, pantry and the kitchen. The pastry house contained boards, shelves, a large chest, and 'a great anvil of iron', which was perhaps used for apprentices to make their 'proof piece' and displayed in the hall on special occasions. The pantry was used to store 30 plates, 30 dishes, 34 saucers, twelve pottagers, six pots and six salts. The kitchen too had boards and shelves, a couple of ladders, two iron spits (the gift of Cornelius Arnold), a large brass pot, a ewer, a diaper table cloth, and a ceremonial drinking cup, made of wood and decorated with silver, known as a maser. This was the gift of 'Maistre Clampard' and its decoration included an image of St Loy.

The appraisers of the inventory also listed miscellaneous items without specifying where they were kept. These included two other masers donated by John Spakman, one of which was adorned with the image of St Loy, and a piece of silver engraved with a rose and a sun, the gift of Isabel Spakman. Another maser bore the name of its donor, Hugh Masterson. The various coverings included two diaper table cloths, two plain table cloths, an old table cloth, two diaper towels, two diaper cupboard cloths, two plain cupboard cloths, and a dozen plain napkins (the gift of Alice Crocherd, the Master's wife). At that time, cupboards were simply boards on which cups were placed. Nearby, were six dozen trenchers (wooden plates). A great chest made of elm, 7½ feet long, was secured by three locks whose keys were kept by the Master and Wardens; inside was a square box that was also locked, containing the money box. A second elm chest, five feet long, one foot wide and one foot high, was another gift of John Crocherd. The remaining items were 'a good tin' and a 'tin pan of iron two yards long, a foot broad and four inches deep'.

The accounts of the Master and Wardens of the Blacksmiths' Company survive from about the same time as the lease. Perhaps this was no coincidence, for if the Company had only just acquired the Hall it now had a place to keep its records, together with its funds and treasures. When a livery company acquired a hall it needed to appoint a Beadle to look after the records, collect the quarterly subscriptions, organise the feasts, keep lists of members and summon them to meetings. Later on, perhaps once they were incorporated by royal charter, companies began to employ a Learned Clerk to keep their records and to provide legal advice; the Beadle was then second in command. However, although their Yeomanry had a Beadle in 1434, the Blacksmiths' Company do not appear to have appointed one until 1569, two years before the grant of their first royal charter. The usual arrangement before then is illustrated by an entry in the accounts for 1547: 'to the clerke of Mary Maudlens for the making of the book of ordinances of the Blacksmiths Spurriers, 5s.'

The earliest surviving accounts in a bound volume that is now kept at the Guildhall include payments for the repair of the Hall over a three-year period and for the rent of a tent next to it. They also acknowledge the payment of rent by Thomas Rogers for 'his dwelling within the hall' during the previous two years. Masons and labourers were paid for 'the new chimneys made in the house next to the hall' before Roger Redgate became tenant. More money was spent on bricks, sand, loam and lime when Thomas Hartlowe, mason, worked on the corbels, mantles and border stones of the chimneys. The insertion of brick chimneys in place of central hearths and louvres in the roof was one of the general improvements to substantial buildings in the Tudor age. The central body of the Hall was now provided with a 'hearth made new of freestone', the floor was paved with tiles, and a new cupboard was installed to store the banners and images. In the years immediately after the taking of the new lease, it is clear that the old building was improved to contemporary standards of comfort. Plays based on stories from the Bible were held on Quarter Days, when subscriptions were due. The London livery companies did not have their own drama tradition but paid visiting players to perform.

The accounts also show that a fee was paid to one of the Greyfriars of Newgate for conducting 'a dirige and mass of requiem' on St Andrew's day and that John Walter was fined for not attending the mass of requiem 'done for the wife of John Wharton'. Payments were also made to a wax chandler for providing the torches that were carried in funeral processions to St Mary Magdalene's Church in Old Fish Street. Another regular entry that appears in 1533 reads: 'paid on St Loy's day for the dinner for the company, £9'.

These early accounts note also the fines that were paid when members of the Company did not dine with the Mayor nor with the Sheriff. Payments were made on these occasions for the hire of a barge and for the wages of the bargemen who rowed representatives of the Company up and down the Thames in the processions associated with these feasts. The Company provided some of its freemen with loans of money or articles, including anvils, and amongst the quarterly payments from members were some from 'foreign brethren', that is blacksmiths who lived and worked beyond the four-mile limit around the City of London. At the same time, the Company sought to prevent 'strangers', or non-members, from selling their wares. With this in mind, they Blacksmiths paid the clerk of the Skinners' Company to make a copy of an Act of King Edward III against 'strangers artificers'. At this time, they clearly did not have a clerk of their own.

The picture of the Blacksmiths' Company in its formative years that can be drawn from the surviving medieval documents is far from complete, but we can see that, in common with the other London livery companies, the Blacksmiths were concerned to preserve their standard of living by enforcing a monopoly of their trade within the City and its suburbs. Their aims were to maintain what they regarded as a just price for their products, to ensure their reputation for making good-quality goods, to restrict entry to the trade through a seven-year apprenticeship system leading to the freedom of the Company, and to stop non-members from underselling them. At the same time, the Company acted as a social organisation which gave its members a strong sense of belonging by arranging feasts and processions and by providing financial help for those who had fallen on hard times. The Company also had an important religious dimension with a patron saint and a regular connection with a local church. The fraternity of the brethren and sisters of St Loy brought the Blacksmiths and their wives together in a way that was probably even more important to them than the pursuit of an economic advantage, though the distinction between these activities would not have occurred to them. The dissolution of these fraternities at the Reformation is a major dividing line between the medieval livery companies and their successors from the reign of Queen Elizabeth I onwards.

The Chartered Company 2

In 1532, according to John Stow's *Survey of London* (1598), the Wardens of the Blacksmiths' Company were ranked 54th in the list of the 60 livery companies in attendance at the Lord Mayor's Feast in the Guildhall. The Blacksmiths' Company was clearly of small significance compared with those of the wealthiest tradesmen and craftsmen of late-medieval London. Even so, when King Henry VIII sought finance from the livery companies for his wars with France and Scotland the Blacksmiths were made to purchase arms, help pay wages, and allow soldiers to be billeted in their Hall. Although they possessed few articles of silver plate, the Wardens were forced to sell some in order to provide 'the King's money'. Further money was 'seized among the Craft of Blacksmiths of London at My Lord Mayor's commandment'. In the days before the country had a standing army and when taxation consisted of arbitrary 'forced loans' and 'subsidies' the Crown saw rich pickings in the common funds of the London livery companies. After all, they could argue, it was in the companies' interest to make sure that the capital city was well protected.

Henry's foreign wars were so unpopular that he stopped this particular imposition, but it was revived in later years by his son, King Edward VI, and his daughters, Queen Mary and Queen Elizabeth I. In 1547 the Blacksmiths' Company paid for a new harness, with buckles and leather, two new bows, seven new arrows, and the feathering of four sheaves of arrows. In the next two years the Company bought two guns, four swords, and a new staff for a bill that was broken. Perhaps these were used in processions rather than for military purposes, but in 1557 the Company spent £2 1s. 6d. on arming and clothing soldiers, probably for service in the Low Countries, and similar payments often appear in the few accounts that survive for the second half of the sixteenth century. In 1558–59 'payments for setting forth of soldiers at sundry times' amounted to £9 5s. 2d., and in September 1601 the Deputy of the

The Blacksmiths' Cup. This Silver Cup was the gift of Christopher Pym, the Clerk of the Company, in 1655, and was the Company's greatest treasure. It was sold in 1785 at the lowest ebb of the Company's fortunes, when the Company abandoned its Hall, but in 1976 Lady Brabourne generously returned it, for display at the London Museum. The Cup is now kept at the Ashmolean Museum, Oxford.

Ward of Queenhithe was paid for 'one half subsidy for setting forth soldiers to Ostend, and building the galley'.

Dissolution of the Fraternity

King Henry VIII's dissolution of the monasteries and his confiscation of their wealth, followed early in King Edward VI's reign by the destruction of chantry chapels and hospitals and the appropriation of their properties, had an enormous impact on the spiritual life, economy and physical appearance of London. The large Franciscan friary that dominated the north-western corner of the city, and which had been the venue for the Blacksmiths' annual procession to attend a dirige and mass of requiem on St Andrew's day, was demolished and its large, valuable site with gardens stretching back to the city wall became the property of the Crown. In 1547 an Act of Parliament, promoted by King Edward VI's government, condemned the 'superstition and errors in Christian religion' created by 'vain opinions of purgatory and masses satisfactory'. The saying of masses for the dead was prohibited, altars dedicated to saints were banned, and all images of the 'holy company of Heaven', including carvings, pictures and stained glass windows, were removed from parish churches throughout the land, including the 100 or so churches within the walls of the City of London.

Crucially for the London livery companies, the 1547 Act also abolished all religious 'fraternities, brotherhoods and guilds', including that of St Loy. This was a savage blow to the religious and social life of men and women throughout the land. The Crown took over all the lands, valued collectively at about £939 per annum, that the various London livery companies had held 'for superstitious purposes'. The fraternity of St Loy did not have any property for the Crown to grab, but its annual procession and the feast day came to an end and, in time, the Blacksmiths' Hall was adorned with the Company's Arms rather than with images of St Loy. The only note in the Company's records that was relevant to these momentous events is the payment of five shillings to Father Johnson as a reward for his good counsel. What that advice was concerned with we do not know, but the note shows that the Wardens valued a connection with the Franciscan friars even after their order had been banned and their property appropriated.

The destruction of the religious fraternity dedicated to St Loy, the patron saint of blacksmiths, marked the end of the medieval era in the Company's long history. From now onwards, civic life in London shifted from the religious to the secular. Yet this transformation provoked little or no resistance. There were no bitter complaints entered into the Company's records. The London livery companies, shorn of their religious function, continued to play an important role in the social as well as the economic life of the City. They still provided feasts for their members on fixed occasions, they managed their properties and charitable bequests, and they pursued their members' economic interests vigorously.

The Blacksmiths' Company continued to express its loyalty to the Crown at special events. The accounts of 'the Wardens of the Craft or Mystery of the Blacksmiths Spurriers' for 1547–48, the first year of the reign of the young King Edward VI, include a payment 'for a rail and setting up thereof when the King's Grace came through London in Gracechurch Street between the Bell and the Cross Keys'. The company were also present in the adjoining Lombard Street on Trinity Sunday, 'afore the King's coming', so this district within Cornhill Ward must still have had particular associations for the Blacksmiths. The last St Andrew's day observation of the dirige was followed by a suitably restrained meal in the Blacksmiths' Hall. The accounts record payments for three dozen white buns, six dozen spiced buns, a kilderkin or small barrel of ale, four cheeses, four pounds of sugar, a quarter of pepper, half an ounce of saffron, an ounce and more of cloves, six pounds of butter, ale for the spiced bread, and coals and candles to warm and light the Hall. Payments were also made for wax torches, or cressets as they were known: 'Paid for 34 stones of cresset lights. Paid to six cresset bearers and to two bag bearers. Paid for food and drink upon the cresset bearers and bag bearers for two nights'. All this now came to an end.

The Hall and Other Properties

During these same years, extensive alterations were made to the Hall. No less than ten pages of the Company's accounts are devoted to small payments for repairs and replacements. This work on the Hall explains why the Wardens and Assistants met and dined at local inns: the Swan in Fish Street, the Boar's Head, and the George. The 1550–52 accounts of the four new Wardens and Assistants also mention the Bull's Head in Cheap and the Saracen's Head at Aldgate. By then, the Hall was back in regular use. The accounts read: 'Paid at the Hall for bread, beer and wine upon Mary Magdalene day, 4*d*.' The catering for the Company's dinner in 1552 is itemised in full:

bread, a barrel of strong beer, a stand of ale; beer, bread and ale for the cook; roses and lavender, a garland of flowers, wine both claret and French; two dozen of trenchers, brooms, linen and caps; a strainer for the cook, two servers for the butlers; a pound and a half of pepper, eight pound of great raisins, two ounce of cloves and mace, saffron, a quarter of a pound of cinnamon, a quarter of a pound of ginger, four pounds of currants, 28 pounds of prunes, a pound of biscuits and caraway, five pounds of sugar; 50 eggs, two dozen geese, three dozen rabbits, legs of veal, eight hinder quarters of mutton, twelve marybones [chicken marrow], half a sirloin of beef, twenty pounds of suet; sturgeon, two fresh salmons, ten capons, two bushels of meal; butter, water for the dressing of the dinner, eight garnish of vessels; a peck of salt, fine salt, a bottle of white vinegar, mustard, red vinegar; four sacks of coals, billet [firewood], half a hundredweight of faggot, three pounds of candles, a quire of paper, rushes, sand; paid for the cook, £1 6s. 8d., a reward for the cook, 3s., paid for the minstrels, 8s., paid to the porter, 8d., paid two women for washing dishes and making clean the house, 8d.

The Company did not yet require the services of a permanent Clerk. Instead, the accounts note: 'Paid to the churchwardens of Mary Magdalene parish for the clerk's wages for one whole year, 4s.' As private charitable donations could no longer be made to monasteries or to chantries and fraternities, such gifts were directed elsewhere. Some of the wealthier London livery companies had long since become the recipients of land held in trust for charitable purposes; such endowments now became more widespread. In order to administer charitable funds, especially those derived from lands that lay well beyond the City's boundaries, livery companies needed to be incorporated by royal charter. When the Blacksmiths' Company began to receive a substantial proportion of its income from the rents of property, it came to see the necessity of applying for a charter of incorporation.

On 3 June 1557 the Company received a legacy from a former Master, when Edward Presteyn, described as 'liveryman of the Company of Blacksmiths and Spurriers of London', bequeathed an inn known as the Crown and Hoop, together with a shop which he had purchased ten years previously, both of which were tenanted by Simon Goldsmith, another former Master of the Blacksmith's Company. These properties stood in the parish of St Sepulchre Without Newgate, near the bars of the Old Bailey and close to Bartholomew's

Hospital in West Smithfield. They remained the Company's chief source of income for charitable purposes until they were sold in 1932. Presteyn's bequest was to enable the Wardens of the Company to 'yearly dispose out of the rents of the said messuage' four shillings 'in charity among the poor Artists of the Society of Blacksmiths and Spurriers'. The Company also received income from the rents of two small properties attached to the Hall.

The Royal Charter of 1571

Two important administrative changes were made during the decade before the Company received its first charter. First, on 5 March 1562 the Mayor and Aldermen of the City approved a petition from 'the Mystery or Company of the Blacksmiths Spurriers of this honourable City' to be known henceforth not as the Blacksmiths Spurriers but simply as The Blacksmiths' Company. This was confirmed by the royal charter of incorporation of 1571. The Spurriers' Company had been formed about 1300, but late in the reign of King Henry VIII they had merged with the Blacksmiths; now they had abandoned their separate identity. Second, on 29 September 1569 John Walton was appointed as the Company's first Beadle. He agreed an annual wage of £3, supplemented by fees of a shilling at each burial and extra payments every time that he notified members about meetings or brought someone before the Court, and at 'the entrance of every man into the clothing'. The position of Clerk was not mentioned in the 1571 charter but it is likely that an appointment was made soon afterwards.

It is unfortunate that the Company's records for most of the reign of Queen Elizabeth I are lost. We have no information about the events leading up to the receipt of the first charter in 1571, nor about the costs involved. The charter informs us that the Blacksmiths and Spurriers 'hath bound and joined … in the name of Blacksmiths only' in 'one body Corporate of four Keepers or Wardens and Society of the Art or Mystery of Blacksmiths London'. Every two years at the feast of the Nativity of Saint John the Baptist (24 June) the Company were to choose 'four of the more ancient and discreet Men' to be Keepers or Wardens for the next two years. This merely codified long-established practice, though in 1394 Election Day had been at Michaelmas (29 September) and accounts continued to start on that day. The 1571 charter enabled the Company to hold property 'for the greater help and sustenance of the poor Men and Women of the Art or Mystery and Society'. In common with other livery companies, their authority over their craft extended 'within the

The King James I Charter. On 21 March 1604 the Company was granted its second charter, confirming that of Queen Elizabeth in 1571. The text is in Latin.

City of London and Suburbs of the same and four miles about the City' and they were given the usual 'full power and lawful authority to observe search rule govern correct and punish'. In particular, 'by virtue of the aforesaid Letters Patent', they were authorised

> to enter into all and all manner of Houses Shops Orchards Cellars Solars and all other places … where any kind of wares used to be

made or wrought by Blacksmiths ... to search try and prove whether any such like wares shall be sufficiently made and wrought and of good and sufficient stuff without any fraud.

This right of search was pursued vigorously until the population of London grew so large in the eighteenth century that it proved impossible to enforce.

The surviving Company's accounts begin again in 1598, when the Wardens dined at The Dagger in Friday Street after viewing their properties. As they were accompanied by a carpenter, we may assume that these houses were timber-framed in the usual manner of London's domestic buildings before the Great Fire of 1666. In the following year, the accounts note that the 'Master and Wardens of the Mystery and Company of the Blacksmiths of the City of London ... received of the gift of Mr Thomas Harpwell, the Lady Howard's porter, a standing silver cup, all gilt'. They also record that the Assistants were each called upon to subscribe towards the provision of sixteen quarters of foreign corn; these subscriptions varied but the highest was £1 and the average was about five shillings. This was a time of national dearth, when corn had to be imported and unusual measures were taken by the Queen's Government to prevent starvation. The bill for the corn was £16, so this was a heavy tax. The Queen also levied occasional forced loans upon the City; all members of the Blacksmiths' Company were called upon to subscribe, but it was still necessary to pay the balance of £32 from the Company's funds. It seems that the Company were able to pay without too much difficulty. During the reign of Queen Elizabeth I the national population recovered to the level it had achieved before the Black Death in the mid-fourteenth century. London grew from an estimated population of 120,000 in 1550 to about 200,000 in 1600, an enormous and rapid advance. Trade flourished and young immigrants poured into the City from all over the land. Shakespeare's London was a vibrant place to be.

In 1601 we find that the Company employed a Clerk at £5 a year, a Beadle at £3, and a Porter for £1. A substantial proportion of the Company's income came from the leases of their properties by the Old Bailey. The 1601–3 accounts, for instance, record that John Lawson paid £50 for a lease and a further £5 10s. 0d. rent, and that William Grainer paid £5, the remainder of an entry fine. When King James I succeeded Queen Elizabeth I to the throne, the Company decided (together with many other bodies up and down the land) that it would safeguard their interests to pay for a royal confirmation of their charter. This was achieved on 21 March 1604. The accounts note: 'Paid for a fine to the King and for the ingrossing and other charges about the confirming of our Charter, £15 7s. 0d.'; other charges and expenses amounted to £9. The Company was prosperous enough to pay these sums without undue concern. The following year, the Blacksmiths joined the other livery companies in welcoming the King of Denmark by erecting stands in Fleet Street and hiring trumpeters. In 1610 they paid Sir William Segar, Garter King of Arms, the principal Herald, £7 12s. 0d. 'for the renewing of the Arms of this Company and to his man and for a dinner'. The motto was changed on this occasion to the present one: 'By hammer and hand all arts do stand'. Nevertheless, the Blacksmiths' remained one of the smaller London livery companies.

A case brought before the Court of Assistants on 28 December 1605 shows the leading men of the Company taking a strong moral line. Roger White and Thomas Wiltshire, two of the Assistants, confessed that 'they went to an Alehouse or Bawdy House and there supped and kept company with lewd women'. They were removed from the Court. On 29 July 1606 the Wardens tried to reinstate them, but all but two of the Assistants voted against the motion. When the Upper Warden put their hoods back on the men's shoulders, the Assistants rose up and left. When the Wardens tried again the following September, the majority of the Assistants remained hostile, whereupon White and Wiltshire 'spake divers evil words and speeches in the Court against those who had put their hands against them. And the said Wiltshire in violent and outrageous manner rushed in among the Assistants and took his place as it were in despite of the Court whereupon the Assistants being displeased thereat rose up'. Eventually, they were both re-admitted and in time Thomas Wiltshire became the junior Warden; it seems that he died before he could rise even further in the ranks of the Company.

When King James I established a Protestant settlement in the six counties of Ulster he imposed a payment of £40,000 upon the City of London livery companies to finance his scheme. On 19 January 1609 the Blacksmiths' Court met to discuss 'the Lord Mayor's precept to take and accept a proportionable share of lands in the province of Ulster … in lieu of the moneys by them already disbursed or hereafter to be disbursed towards the Plantation … so to build and plant the same at their costs and charges'. They asked for more time, but ten days later were forced to make a first payment 'towards the Plantation in Ireland according to the Lord Mayor's precept for £32'. In 1611 the Assistants and Livery subscribed £33 16s. 3d. and the Yeomanry contributed £33 10s. 1d. The £40,000 that the king demanded was divided into twelve equal portions, each under the leadership of one of the twelve

Set of four goblets for the Wardens, engraved with the Company's Arms. They were presented by Prime Warden Norman Iles to commemorate the quatro-centenary of the first Charter, granted by Queen Elizabeth I in 1571.

Great Companies. The Blacksmiths' Company was amongst a group of neighbouring smaller ones that were placed under the control of the Vintners' Company, whose Hall was near the Thames a little further east from Lambeth Hill, in Vintry Ward.

Relationships with other companies were sometimes fractious as each fought to protect their own interests and authority. The Blacksmiths' Company was prepared to spend large sums of money on litigation in pursuit of its causes. At the beginning of the seventeenth century the Wardens were in dispute with the Armourers' Company, and in 1609–10 payments amounting to £26 1s. 6d. were made to defend four members 'who used the trade of Farriers from being disfranchised at the suit of the Company of Farriers'. At the same time, the Blacksmiths paid £3 at 'divers meetings and for divers dinners' to consider the suit of the Woodmongers, who wanted to transfer to their membership William Stephens, 'free of this Company that goeth with a cart'. We do not know the outcome of this case, but wrangles over freemen transferring from one trade and company to another became increasingly common as the century progressed. In 1631, after long arguments, the Clockmakers left the Blacksmiths' Company to form their own organisation, and in 1639 the Blacksmiths' Wardens were called to attend the Right Honourable the Lord Keeper 'to answer the Clockmakers and Gunsmiths petition by Counsel'. In the same year, support was given to the spurriers within the Blacksmiths' Company who were prosecuting other spurriers 'that use that art having not gowned for it', that is not having gone to the expense of joining the livery.

The Liverymen of the Blacksmiths' Company were the better-off masters who supported the Wardens and Assistants and attended the dinners. The younger freemen who were starting up in the trade, together with the large numbers of journeymen and servants who worked for wages, continued to form a second rank within the Company, known as the Yeomanry. They appear only fleetingly in the records of the Blacksmiths' Company; for example, the accounts of 1611–13 note the payment of Quarterage (quarterly subscriptions) by the Yeomanry. The members of this junior body were welcomed by their seniors, for they could provide useful information about the talk in the trade, problems that were arising, and the latest deceptions. In particular, they could point to abuses when searches were made to ensure the quality of goods and adherence to the Company's ordinances. It was expected that young freemen would eventually move up to the livery. Josias Devoris, who was a member of the Yeomanry in 1611–13, rose to be Upper Warden of the Company in 1639. However, those who remained journeymen or servants never made this upward step and stayed within the Yeomanry all their lives. In 1661, for example, Edward Rott pleaded to be excused from the expense of being 'one of the Stewards for the next Yeomanry Dinner' on the grounds that 'he was antient, and had little or no trade'. After 'serious debate', the Company discharged him upon payment of the hefty sum of £5. Refusal to hold office, on account of the expense, was a matter of on-going concern. In 1647, for instance, six members of the Yeomanry within the Blacksmiths' Company were each fined £4 for declining to become stewards at the annual dinner.

The large number of admissions that were entered into the Company's registers suggest that the Blacksmiths were doing well at this time. The accounts for 1615–17 show that they could readily afford to buy new silver plate, including 'a Double Bell Salt chased and gilt weighing 18¾ ounces, also a double White salt with open cover, three white beer bowls, three wine bowls and three smaller wine bowls'. The fashion for three-tiered 'bell' salts to place on the high table at feasts began about the end of the sixteenth century, but did not last long. This prosperity enabled the Company to invest in property. On 1 March 1636 the 'Keeper or Wardens and Society of the Art or Mystery of Blacksmiths London' made an investment of lasting value, when they paid Richard Goswell of Chickenden (Oxfordshire) £270 for:

> All those three messuages or tenements as they were then situate lying and being in the parish of St Andrews next Baynards Castle ... abutting on the Church Yard of the said parish church on the east and the King's highway leading to Puddle Wharf on the west, and on a messuage or tenement of the said Richard Goswell and Mary his wife being a tavern and known by the sign of the Queen's Head on the north and on the messuage or tenement of Humphrey Lee then in the occupation of Samuel Jones, feltmaker, on the south.

The cost of building new houses on this site brought the final expenditure to £378 2s. 6d. Four years later, on 24 March 1640, the Blacksmiths' Company purchased Goswell's other four adjoining properties, including the Queen's Head tavern, so it then had seven messuages or tenements there.

The Company's accounts for the first half of the seventeenth century note several gifts and bequests. In 1615–17 a beaker was donated by Mr Starkey, a former Upper Warden, and engraved at the cost of the Company. On 20 January 1631 a new Clerk, Michael Pym, gentleman, a Clerk in the Lord Mayor's Court, was elected and six days later admitted as a brother of the Company. In return, Pym presented a basin and ewer of silver with the Company's arms engraved, priced at £23 13s. 0d. He no doubt continued to do other lucrative legal work in addition to his duties with the Company. Among the legacies that were received, William Pierce, a former freeman, bequeathed £12 to be lent out from time to time to three poor smiths, and Roger Harris, a former Clerk, left £6 for a similar purpose to two more poor freemen. In 1661, when 'Mr Warden Currier' augmented these gifts with a further £7, a table of legacies was hung in the Hall. The Company received another bequest the following year when Francis Kirkman donated a silver tankard.

The loss of the Company's records for most of the reign of Queen Elizabeth I prevents us from discovering when the leading Warden first became known as Upper Warden rather than Master, but it seems that the process was a gradual and muddled one rather than the result of a deliberate decision. When the accounts re-start in 1599–1601 they refer to the Upper Warden and three Wardens. Confusingly, at the Court of Assistants held at the Blacksmiths' Hall on 6 June 1605 Mr Hollis was recorded as Master, Mr Bickford as Upper Warden, and Mr Powell as Third Warden, but this is the only occasion when the second warden in seniority was recorded as the Upper Warden. In 1629 reference was made, in the old manner, to the

Master, Wardens and Assistants, and in 1634 it was agreed that 'The Master and Wardens shall proceed in the obtaining of a longer lease from the City of the Company's Hall and shall do so for the covenanting to new build as to them shall seem meet'. Then on 2 August 1638 Mr Shaw, the Upper Warden, asked to be relieved of the post because his continual attendance at St Paul's Cathedral, where he was the master smith, 'taketh up all his time'. In agreeing to his discharge, the Company noted that, 'There is a recent cause to have an Upper Warden who anciently hath been called the Master'. We can conclude therefore that Upper Warden had gradually become the accepted term, without any formal decision to that effect.

Puritan Influence

By the reign of King Charles I the leading members of the Blacksmiths' Company, in common with those of many of the City's other livery companies, held very different religious views from those of their medieval predecessors. The days of sacred processions, following banners and torches to the Greyfriars church, had long since passed, but the Company still paid for a sermon at their feast and sometimes assembled in a parish church. By the 1630s, if not before, the Wardens and Assistants of the Blacksmiths' Company were men who favoured the Puritan cause in thinking that the reform of religion had not gone far enough. This explains their apparently callous behaviour towards Mr Matthew Griffith, the parson of St Mary Magdalene's church in Old Fish Street. This church stood just up the road from the Blacksmiths' Hall and the Company had long regarded it as their spiritual home, even though they were no longer allowed to have a dedicated altar there. In 1630 the Company's accounts record a payment of £2 to Mr Griffith, 'given as a gratuity or benevolence upon request made by him for the same and not in respect of duty or increase of his tithes'. The account noted that the gift was 'thankfully accepted'. This is the first hint of trouble and the records for the years 1635–37 show that the relationship between the Company and Mr Griffith quickly turned sour. In a bitter letter, which was copied into the Company's records, the parson complained that he had not been asked to give a sermon 'these last four years', nor had he received any offering, 'so I have had nothing but bare two shillings a quarter for tithes of the hall, which is one of the best houses in my parish and yields me not a penny in a year any other way'. He recounted that he had visited the Blacksmiths' Hall to put his case, but the Wardens and Assistants had merely sent their 'alms man' to know his business. In an extraordinary outburst he wrote, 'I should have looked for better respect from some of you who are zealous professors, but that I know you are all but Blacksmiths and show your breeding and how well you love the Church. St Paul suffered much under Demetrius the silversmith and by Alexander the coppersmith and it is my unhappiness to fall into the hands of the Blacksmiths.'

The jibe that 'some of you' were 'zealous professors', even though they were only humble craftsmen, provides the clue that influential members of the Company were Puritans. With this in mind, we can see that their support for a young clergyman, John Hodges, was not simply because he was the son of 'a brother of this Company'. In 1629 they granted Hodges an exhibition of £2 a year for each of the three years that he was a scholar at Trinity College, Oxford, whose President, Robert Harris, was an influential Puritan. When he graduated as a Master of Arts, Hodges was given a £1 gratuity. The Company's accounts of 1637–39 note further that he was paid for giving a sermon at St Anne's, Blackfriars in the Ward of Faringdon Within, where he had been appointed to the living. St Anne's was a relatively new church, consecrated in 1597, which had become a well-known Puritan stronghold within the City. It is clear where the allegiances of the leading members of the Blacksmiths' Company lay. Meanwhile, Matthew Griffith failed to attract a congregation of Blacksmiths in their old parish church of St Mary Magdalene's. In 1643, when the Civil War was well underway and the Roundheads were in control in London, Parliament issued an order:

> for sequestering the rents and profits of the parsonage of St. Mary Magdalene's, near Old Fish Street, where Mr. Matthew Griffith was parson, into the hands of certain sequestrators named in the said ordinance; and for putting in of Ithiell Smart, Master of Arts, a godly, learned, and orthodox divine; who is thereby required to preach every Lord's Day, and to officiate as parson, and to take care for the discharge of the cure of the said place in all the duties thereof, until further order be taken by both Houses of Parliament, was this day read; and, by vote upon the question, assented unto; and ordered to be sent unto the Lords for their concurrence.

It was resolved further that 'Mr. Matthew Griffith be forthwith sent for, as a delinquent, by the Serjeant at Arms, attending on this House'. Having got a preacher whose opinions they agreed with, the liverymen of the Blacksmiths' Company were now able to worship again at St Mary Magdalene's. Their strong interest in reformed religion is also apparent from the gift of £4 in 1634 to St Alban's Church, Wood Street, which had fallen into disrepair and was completely rebuilt, and from a contribution of £16 towards the repair of St Paul's Cathedral. This interest is also evident in a record dated 29 July 1646, when their Clerk, Michael Pym, presented the Court of the Blacksmiths' Company with a book of divinity, the work of Peter Martyr, a former Italian monk who, in 1547, had become regius professor of divinity at Oxford. The author was a leading religious reformer, much appreciated by the Protestants of his time and by the later Puritans.

The Royal Charter of 1639

On 15 February 1639 the Company renewed the charter that had been granted in 1571 and 'Paid Mr Solicitor his fee for pursuing of our charter and ordinances and his opinion therein, £5'. The decision to seek a new charter was perhaps prompted by disputes with the Clockmakers and Gunsmiths. Four Keepers or Wardens and 21 Assistants were authorised to 'keep and appoint a certain House or Council Hall called the Blacksmiths Hall' and to 'keep a certain Court or Convocation within the same House or Hall for the affairs and business of the said Society'. As the charter remains the one by which the Company is governed, the main articles are worth quoting. They began by confirming 'ancient ordinances' by which every householder of the Company paid 6d. each quarter into the common fund and every journeyman 3d. They repeated that:

> no person or persons whatsoever … within the City of London or within four miles of the same City do use or exercise the Arts or Mysteries aforesaid … unless first he or they shall serve as apprentice or apprentices for the space of seven years in the said several Arts … according to the form of the Statute in the fifth year of the reign of the Lady Elizabeth late Queen [The Statute of Artificers, 1563].

> That no-one shall put his particular mark upon every work or workmanship of his by which the workman of the same wares or workmanship may be discerned. Which mark of every such artificer we will and ordain by these presents to be registered at the Blacksmiths Hall before the Keepers or Wardens of the Society aforesaid in a Register there for this purpose.

And that no dissolute idle or slothful persons within the City of London or within four miles from the same from henceforth shall go about and cry old iron or there to offer to sale any wares to the said Arts or Mysteries belonging (by way of hawking) against the form of the statute.

It was agreed that apprentices of the Armourers' Company in London could be bound to a Blacksmith. This appears to have been a concession that the Blacksmiths' Company had been forced to make.

The ordinances that received official approval two years later stated that the Election Day for Wardens should be on 'the first Thursday next after the feast day of Saint James the Apostle' (25 July), a change from previous practice. The Beadle was to inform each member, in print or writing, at his dwelling house or shop. Members had to arrive at the Common Hall by 8 o'clock in the morning for the election, afterwards 'in decent and comely manner and in his Livery' each freeman was expected to proceed to church to hear a sermon, before returning back to the Hall for a meal. The admission fee to the livery was fixed at £4 'to be employed as a stock for corn to be provided by the said Society as by a precept from the Lord Mayor', an old provision from the 1590s. The Upper Warden, as he was now formally known, the other Wardens, and the Assistants had to wear gowns when they sat in Court, and every Liveryman called to that Court was to be similarly attired. When any Liveryman or his wife died, the Beadle had to summons everyone to 'accompany the corpse to the grave'. The ordinances thus kept alive some of the old medieval customs. During the Civil War, however, when 'the times [were] very hard and trading dead', it was agreed in January 1646 to reduce the cost of the cloth worn at funerals.

One of the powers confirmed by the charter was that of search to ensure the quality of the goods produced by members of the Company and to root out the work of 'strangers' who did not belong. The right to 'enter into all and all manner of Houses Shops Orchards Cellars Solars and all other places whatsoever' was exercised well into the eighteenth century, especially at the annual Bartholomew and Southwark Fairs. From the twelfth century onwards, the Bartholomew Fair at West Smithfield, in the north-western part of the City, had been held on the feast and morrow of St Bartholomew (24–25 August), but it had become a great pleasure fair as well as a commercial event and in King Charles II's reign it was extended to a fortnight. Southwark Fair, which was originally held from 7 to 9 September, was likewise lengthened to a full two weeks. The 1641 ordinances described this power of search as the right to enter 'every or any Market Fair House Shop Warehouse used or occupied by any of the said Corporation or by any using the said Art of a Blacksmith or a Spurrier within the … City of London and Suburbs thereof or within four miles of the said City'. An earlier order made in April 1632 for 'trial of guns' illustrates the practicalities of such searches: 'Monday next is appointed for to search for insufficient pieces guns and pistols and Wednesday following to try guns pieces and pistols which are already found in the hands and custody of John Robinson and Nicholas Wilkinson and conceived to be insufficient'.

The accounts of the Wardens from St James' day, 25 July 1646, to 19 July 1647 are typical in their layout and their concerns at this time. They begin by noting the receipt of £22 8s. 2d. in subscriptions 'upon Quarter days and other Court days'. But members did not willingly come to the Hall to pay their dues. Instead, the Wardens and officers had to go knocking on doors and visiting stalls at fair times. £9 8s. 1d. was collected in Quarterage during the two General Searches, and a further £9 7s. 6d. at the searches at the Bartholomew and Southwark fairs. Receiving, 'turning over', and approving the proof pieces of apprentices brought in £8 1s. 0d. 'Persons being made free by patrimony and service,' paid £12 8s. 0d. and each of these new freemen presented the Wardens with a customary spoon. Six freemen who went on to join the Livery paid £4 each. Substantial fines for not accepting office came to £39 and small fines for 'neglect' or 'abuses' brought in £2 19s. 0d. The large sum of £77 9s. 0d. was collected from rents of properties, and £30 17s. 0d. was returned by the Mayor and Corporation from previous loans. But in order to meet current expenditure, £155 was borrowed on interest from a man and two women.

On the expenditure side, payments began with annual salaries. The Clerk now received £10, the Beadle £5 and 'for perfecting bills 8s., for cleaning the armour, 6d.', the Beadle's assistant, £2, the Porter £1. Mrs Hollis, the caretaker, received £1 as her salary and a further 15 shillings 'for her pains during the time of the repairing of the Hall', her maid was paid 2s. 6d., and the Cook £1 16s. 8d. 'for dressing dinners'. New books (which survive in the Company's archives) were bought for £1 3s. 8d. to enter details of the apprentices and freemen and to record the accounts. These accounts also noted miscellaneous payments, such as the rent of the Hall £3, the tithes of the Hall eight shillings, the clerk of the church's wages four shillings, the scavenger two shillings, and the stewards of the Mayor's Feast £3, together with four wine barrels £4 7s. 6d. The Lord Mayor's officer received a salary of 13s. 4d. and other small payments when members of the Company attended his Court. The money that was returned in full to 23 Assistants, at 15 shillings each, and 47 Liverymen, at 7s. 6d. each, 'for what they lent for corn', amounted to £34 17s. 6d.

The Company gave £1 2s. 6d. to 'the poor of the parish', £5 to several poor pensioners by quarterly payments, and four shillings to poor members from Mr Presteyn's legacy. Other 'gifts' included five shillings to Christopher Pym (who eventually succeeded his father as the Company's Clerk) and another five shillings 'for his pains in writing the book of apprentices and another of the freemen for 40 years last past'. Mrs Reeve and Widow Norman received five shillings apiece, Mrs Hollis and Mrs Sparkes (the Porter's wife) were given two shillings each, Mrs Hollis's maid 6d., and the Cook's man two shillings. Finally, a generous £3 13s. 6d. was given to Sarah Tailor, the daughter of Mrs Abbot, 'as of the love of the Company'.

Conducting the various searches by the Wardens and the four officers – Clerk, Beadle, Porter, and assistant Beadle – proved time-consuming and cost altogether £15 16s. 5d., including 1s. 4d. for 'leads', which were presumably tips for information about offenders. But the major expense was that of running the Hall and holding events there. The fuel bill for coals, billets, faggots and charcoal came to £3 6s. 0d., 'Hollis and his wife's bills' came to £4 15s. 5d., various 'necessary payments' amounted to £28 9s. 11d., unspecified expenses totalled £15 7s. 8d., and dinners cost the Company £33 0s. 6d. This was a time of unusual expenditure on 'repairs about the Hall' when payments to a carpenter, bricklayer, mason, slater, plumber, paviour, plasterer, and painter, and the cost of tiles, wire, and iron work amounted to £139 5s. 5d.

Apprentices

The Company placed great emphasis on its power to insist on a seven years apprenticeship for boys whose fathers were not Liverymen of at least three years standing. A Liveryman was not allowed to take more than two apprentices at a time. The fee that was payable to the Master upon the formal binding of an apprentice by indenture was determined by the Court of the Company. Upon completing his seven-year term the apprentice had to offer proof of his competence by presenting a piece for examination by the Wardens. If this was approved, he was then eligible for the freedom of the Company. The Blacksmiths' apprenticeship registers at the Guildhall are amongst the best of any of the livery companies. They form a regular series from February 1632 to 1781, with a gap from May 1652 to February 1680. They note the name of the master, the name of the apprentice, and the name, occupation and place of residence of the apprentice's father. An alphabetical index of the 13,227 entries has been compiled by Cliff Webb and published by the Society of Genealogists as Volume 41 of their London Livery Company Apprenticeship Registers. From this, it is possible to extract information about the 1,895 entries from the Blacksmith's Company's first volume, which covers the period February 1632 to May 1652. The information about the place of residence of the apprentice's father is invaluable in showing that boys were attracted to London from just about all over England and many scattered parts of Wales. We do not know the names of the members of the Blacksmiths' Company who were born and bred in London and trained in the craft by their fathers, but it is clear that large numbers of provincial boys flocked to the capital city and formed a substantial part of the workforce. Many of them went on to be freemen and liverymen and some to play an important role in the Company's affairs.

London was the great exception to the general rule that most people stayed within their native districts bounded by their nearest market towns. In the seventeenth century the capital city was connected to market centres in every part of the land by weekly carrying services. Those who could not afford to ride on the carrier's cart could get there by foot. London grew at an astonishing rate, from about 200,000 in 1600 to nearly half a million by 1700. Yet the number of recorded burials in London's 100 or so parishes was consistently greater than the number of recorded baptisms. The city's growth was fuelled by immigration. It has been estimated that the huge rise in London's population between 1650 and 1750 can be accounted for only if the annual number of migrants was at least 8,000. Most of these immigrants were young men and women, as they are today. In 1680 the Yorkshire squire, Sir John Reresby, complained in the House of Commons that 'London drained all England of its people'. London's growth in the seventeenth century was far higher than that of the rest of England. In 1550 only about 4 per cent of the national population lived in the capital city; by 1700 nearly 10 per cent were Londoners. As their surnames showed, the people who settled in the capital city were a rich mixture of people from all over England and from many parts of Wales, Scotland and continental Europe. At any one time, only a minority of Londoners had been born there. The pull of the capital city was exceptional, though the leading provincial cities attracted migrants on a smaller scale. Population levels there were modest in comparison with London. In the late seventeenth century Norwich was the next largest city, with 30,000 inhabitants.

We need to keep in mind that sons of Liverymen did not need to serve a formal apprenticeship, so the large numbers of boys who were born within the City of London or within four miles of its borders were not recorded. We have no way of estimating how many boys became blacksmiths in this way, though undoubtedly their number was considerable. The number of locally born boys whose fathers plied a different trade comprised 204 from the City of London, 160 from Middlesex, and 72 from Surrey (who were largely from Southwark on the south bank of the Thames), a total of 436 apprentices or 23 per cent of the whole number in the period 1632–52. This means, however, that 77 per cent of the apprentices came from much further away. Where did they come from?

Surprisingly few of them came from the counties that lie to the south of London, even those that were not far away. Kent provided only 28 boys and Sussex 15. Further west, similar modest numbers were sent from Hampshire (26), Dorset (12), Somerset (20), Devon (6) and Cornwall (4). Altogether, only 111 apprentices came from these seven southern counties during these 21 years. Nor did many come from Essex and East Anglia. Despite the fact that Essex bordered on London, it provided only 48 boys, Suffolk sent only 10 and Norfolk 17. Likewise, only 16 boys came from neighbouring Huntingdonshire and only 26 travelled the short distance to the capital city from Bedfordshire.

These numbers are modest compared with those from the small towns and countryside of Midland England. Strikingly, by far the largest number from an individual county came from Northamptonshire (199 boys or 10.5 per cent of the total). This was much more than double the number from any other county, except for Middlesex (which was populated largely by the inhabitants of north London suburbs). Next came the neighbouring county to the north, Leicestershire (88). The other adjoining counties also supplied large numbers of apprentices to the Blacksmiths' Company: Oxfordshire (84), Warwickshire (84), Buckinghamshire (78), Gloucestershire (74), Berkshire (74), Wiltshire (64), Hertfordshire (53), and Cambridgeshire (48).

Further west, on the Welsh borders, the numbers of boys who moved to London to serve an apprenticeship with a blacksmith were lower, though they were considerably larger than those from East Anglia: Shropshire (37), Herefordshire (33), Worcestershire (33), and from scattered parts of Wales (41). The north midland apprentices arrived in similar numbers: Nottinghamshire (38), Lincolnshire (25), Derbyshire (22), Staffordshire (20), Cheshire (10), and tiny Rutland (4). In northern England, the three ridings of Yorkshire, which together covered one-eighth of the country, sent 62 boys, Lancashire sent 27, Cumberland 16, Westmorland 9, and Durham 4. Northumberland was the only county in England to provide no apprentices at all for the London blacksmiths during this 21-year period. Three other lads came from Scotland, and one crossed the Irish Sea from Dublin.

How can we explain this varied pattern? In particular, why did so many boys move from Northamptonshire in search of a new life in London? The occupations of the fathers of the apprentices are recorded in all but five of the 199 cases from that county. They included 15 blacksmiths and 50 men who between them pursued 24 different ways of earning a living, but by far the largest number were farmers or farm labourers: 20 were yeomen (the better-off farmers), 91 were husbandmen (the usual term for a small farmer) and 18 were labourers. This means that two out of every three Northamptonshire fathers who apprenticed their sons with London blacksmiths worked on the land; and no doubt some of the neighbouring craftsmen were part-time farmers. This agricultural background in Northamptonshire is more marked than in the country as a whole, where just over 44 per cent of the fathers were farmers or labourers. Most of Northamptonshire, except for small areas within forests or in the fens, formed part of a broad belt, dominated by heavy clays and stretching down from north-east England through the midlands to the Upper Thames Valley, which was farmed on the classic three common-fields system divided into strips. This is where the largest number of deserted medieval villages are found. Northamptonshire, Leicestershire and Warwickshire were the counties that were most involved in the Midland Revolt of 1607, when local people rose in arms to destroy the new hedged enclosures whereby unscrupulous men had taken away their precious common pastures and had thus deprived them of vital grazing rights. The farmers of these counties found themselves in a stressful situation in the first half of the seventeenth century. They seem to have advised their sons – perhaps particularly younger sons with no land to inherit – that their best course would be to join the rising numbers of boys who sought a very different type of living in London. Most of the apprentices who moved to London seem to have found their masters with the help of 'friends', older men who were relatives or godparents, or who were sometimes connected with the father socially or through business. Most provincial families had at least one friend in London who would negotiate on their behalf, and some had several.

Detail of a map drawn by Richard Newcourt and engraved by William Faithorne in 1658. The buildings are not depicted accurately, but the position of the Blacksmiths' Hall, south of St Paul's Cathedral, is seen within the tightly packed landscape of the City of London.
© THE BRITISH LIBRARY BOARD, MAPS, CRACE I, 35

Renovating the Hall

During the 1650s the Company spent a lot of money on decorating its Hall on Lambeth Hill. Work began in January 1651, when the Porter was paid three shillings for whitewashing 'the Late King's Armes in the Hall', that is two years after Charles I's execution, but this image with the Company's Arms was not replaced until the summer of 1657. We get an impression of a building that was rather cluttered at times. In October 1652, for instance, the Beadle was allowed to live in rooms next to the Armoury until he could find something more suitable; he was paid regularly for cleaning the weapons in the Armoury. The external appearance of the Hall was unprepossessing, for houses belonging to the Company were built right up to it. In December 1656 leases for two of these houses, 'in Lambeth Hill, adjoining the hall', brought the Company £60 and £50 respectively.

About this time, the Company paid the City Corporation £300 for a new lease of the site for 61 years. They then resolved to improve the appearance of the Hall. In June 1657 John Pierce, a member of the Painter-Stainers' company, was paid £10 to decorate the main rooms and Thomas Townsrow, a plasterer, was paid £10:

> to whiten the Hall inside and outside and all the rooms belonging to it, and to wash and stop the same where occasion is. And all the timbers to be blacked, traced with yellow, and on each side blue. The stairs going up to the Parlour as they are now. And the bottoms of the entry in tracery.

That same month, it was ordered 'that the brick wall and the banks of earth in the yard should be taken down and the ground laid level, and the same ground be railed. And the rails laid in oil'. Payments for other improvements to the hall and parlour continued throughout the summer of 1657: stones were purchased to improve the entrance; the clock case was given a new pane; and the Company's Arms in the glass window in the parlour was protected with wire.

The renovations were completed in time for the Blacksmiths' Feast on Election Day, 25 July 1657. All the Wardens, Assistants, Liverymen and their wives were invited 'according to ancient custom' to the now brightly coloured hall. On display was the silver Blacksmiths' Cup, the gift in January 1656 of Christopher Pym upon his appointment as the Company's Clerk, as the successor to his father. The cup stands about a foot high and its distinctive feature is the figure of Vulcan on the stem. Every couple were asked to pay 2s. 6d. for the meal; the rest of the cost was met from the Company's funds. As the accounts note that twenty dozen trenchers were provided, the entire gathering must have numbered up to 240. They would have been rather squashed together on the benches around the tables. After the meal, a sermon was delivered, 'as was heretofore usual', for which the minister was paid £1. The musicians who entertained the Company from the gallery received £1 10s. 0d.

The dinner may be compared with that of 1552, noted above. The accounts record payments for a barrel of strong beer, a barrel of small beer, and a kilderkin of ale, amounting to £1 7s. 0d. Payments for fuel in the form of billets, faggots, small coal, charcoal and the cost of bringing them in, came to £1 9s. 4d., with an extra 17 shillings for 17 dozen of faggots. The beef cost 12s. 6d. and 'for its porterage' 1s. 4d., and the bread cost £1. The cook served fourteen messes of meat, each of which provided a group of about sixteen people with the following dishes: six boiled chickens in a dish, a giggett (or leg) of mutton, a patty of mutton, a goose, a capon and a codling tart; with the 'fancies and dressing' these cost £24 4s. 8d. The vintner was paid £3 7s. 4d. and nosegays and twinings cost 5s. 6d. The poor at the door were given two shillings between them.

The Company now had a brightly coloured and well-lit Hall that had been brought up to date and of which is liverymen could be proud. They had occupied it for at least 160 years and perhaps much longer. Their future seemed secure, but within a decade of this feast the building was burned to the ground in the Great Fire of London.

The Quest House. After the Great Fire of 1666 had destroyed the Blacksmiths' Hall, the Company leased the Quest House standing by St Giles, Cripplegate for a few years until their new Hall was ready. The Quest House was demolished in 1903.

The New Blacksmiths' Hall   3

During the years following the execution of King Charles I and the rise to power of Oliver Cromwell as Lord Protector, the Blacksmiths' Company continued to meet socially and to look after its members' interests in time-honoured fashion. On 8 February 1654, for example, the Livery of the Company, in accordance with the Lord Mayor's command, assembled in their best gowns and hoods, with their streamers and banners, as Lord Protector Cromwell's procession wound its way to a feast at the Grocers' Hall with the Lord Mayor. That October, as usual, the Company took part in the Lord Mayor's Show, when a barge was hired for the procession up the River Thames to Westminster. And in 1659 a silver staff head, inscribed with the Company's motto, 'By hammer and hand all arts do stand', was made for the Beadle in time for that year's Show.

The Blacksmiths Company responded to the general enthusiasm when the monarchy was restored the following year. On 4 May 1660 the Lord Mayor was given £24 as the Company's two per cent proportion of the £1,200 present from the City to 'the King's Most Excellent Majesty'. The Clerk and sixteen leading members of the Company took the Oath of Allegiance and Supremacy and on 11 November 1660 the Company paid 'for painting the Parlour Chimney, and Andirons, and getting up the King's Arms' in their Hall and for 'painting the King's Arms and a frame for the cloth'.

Plague and Fire

In the early years of King Charles II's reign, the City of London was hit by two major disasters: plague and fire. London had long been notoriously unhealthy. Back in the early sixteenth century, this 'stinking city' had been described by a foreigner as 'the filthiest of the world'. Plague was endemic and the capital had suffered from four other major outbreaks of the disease

Detail of John Ogilby and William Morgan, A Large and Accurate Map of the City of London (1676), taken ten years after the Great Fire. Much of the City of London had already been rebuilt. The Blacksmiths' Hall is shown (left centre), near St Mary Magdalene's churchyard. The church itself stood at the junction of Lambeth Hill and Old Fish Street.

© THE BRITISH LIBRARY BOARD, MAPS, CRACE II, 61

between 1563 and 1636; indeed, the plagues of 1563 and 1603 killed a higher proportion of the metropolitan population than that of 1665, though the last outbreak claimed higher numbers as the total number of inhabitants was then much larger. In two long periods between 1606 and 1610 and between 1640 and 1647 plague accounted for more than ten per cent of London's recorded burials every year. The 1665 epidemic started in the slums of St Giles-in-the-Fields and spread to the parishes inside the north-western walls of the City. One of the parishes that was hit worst was St Michael's Cornhill, where many blacksmiths lived and worked in overcrowded conditions. At the height of the 1665 epidemic over 50 people were buried each day in several of the larger parishes on the fringes of the City.

The Great Fire in the following year was the most momentous event in London's long history. It started at a bakery in Pudding Lane shortly after midnight on Sunday 2 September 1666 and spread rapidly west. Soon, strong winds from the east turned it into a conflagration. By Wednesday, seven out of every eight buildings in the City, and all those immediately to the west of the medieval walls, had been gutted. The surviving houses and public buildings were huddled together inside the northern wall. About 13,200 houses, 87 parish churches, St Paul's Cathedral, and all the halls of the City's livery companies were destroyed. The Blacksmiths' Hall and the Company's other leasehold properties had been consumed by the Fire during the second day.

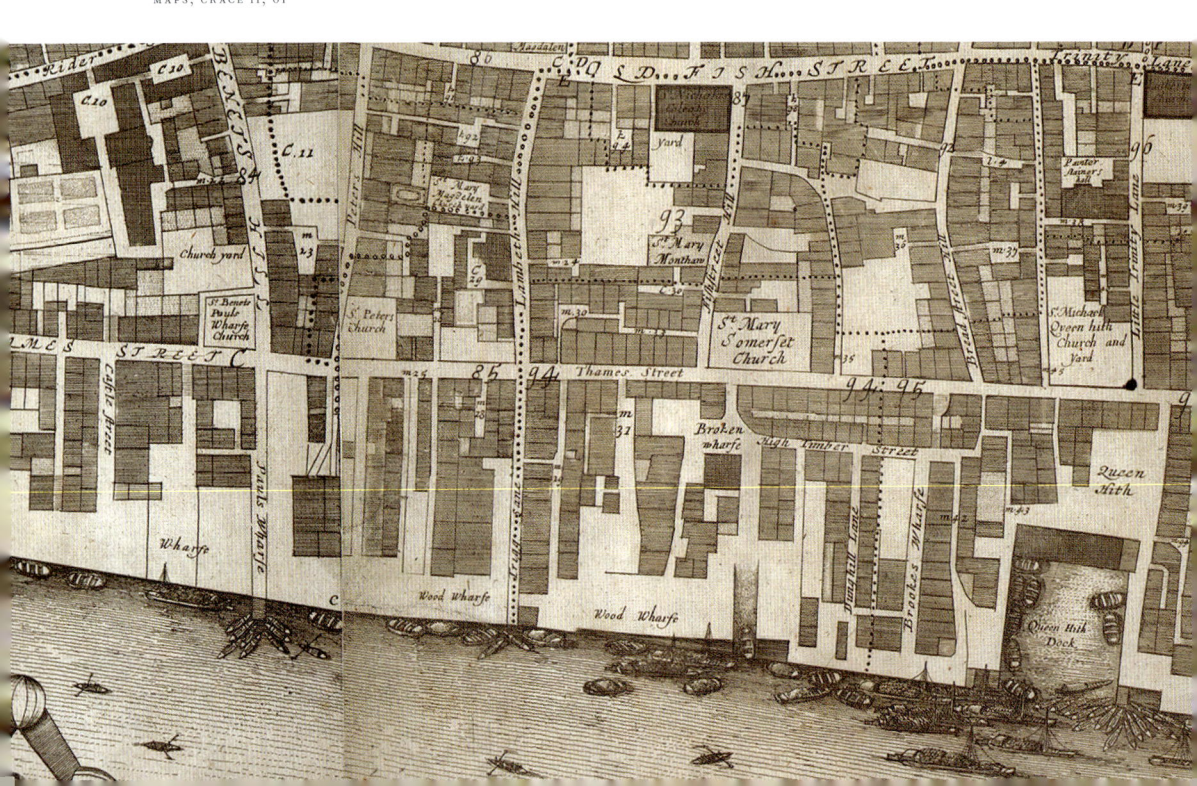

The Blacksmiths' Chest. The Company's accounts for 1667–68 note that £7 5s. 0d. was 'Paid for a chest with three locks and a till in it with a lock, wherein to put the plate, money and writings'. The three locks, opened with different keys, by three wardens, are the main features of the chest. The sides of the chest were made from a single piece of pine that was about 150–200 years old. References in the Company's archives for 1701 and 1786 show that the chest was stored at the Guildhall. Since its restoration by Liveryman Paul Allen it has been kept at the Painters' Hall.

There had just been time to remove the Company's treasures and archives. The accounts read: 'Paid for removing the Linnen, Pewter, Plate, Writings, Books, and other things from the Hall in the time of the late dreadful fire, £7 6s. 0d.' It seems, however, that the venerable chest was consumed by the flames.

In the aftermath of the Fire, the Company were able to secure, for occasional use, a short lease of a share of a building known as the Quest House, which had been erected ten years earlier against the church of St Giles Cripplegate, just outside the City Wall in an area which had escaped the Fire. The medieval church survives amidst the present Barbican complex. The Quest House and four adjoining shops were demolished in 1903, but its appearance is known from a photograph. The Company paid an annual rent of £6 for their use of a room until their new Hall was completed several years later.

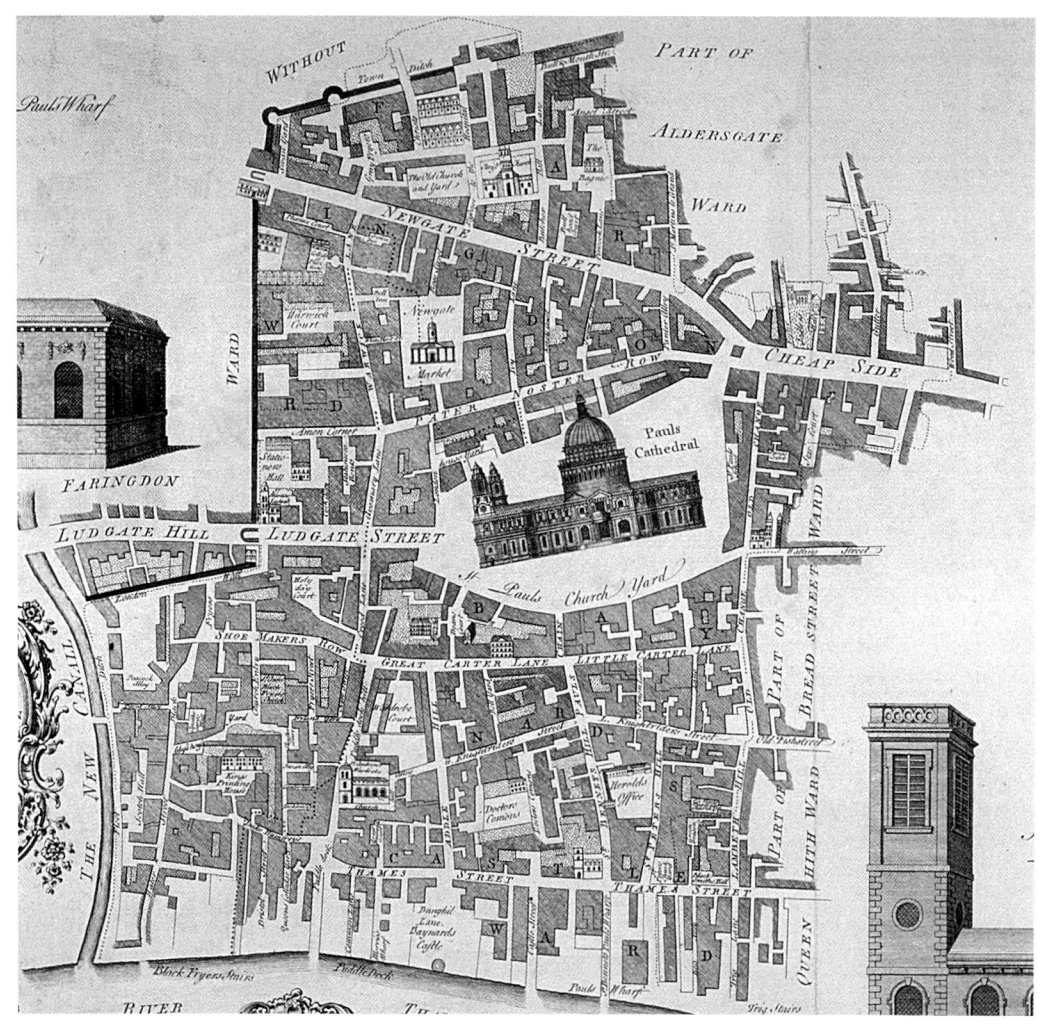

Map of Baynard Castle Ward and Faringdon Ward Within, surveyed by Benjamin Cole for William Maitland, *History of London* (1756). The Blacksmiths' Hall, which lay right on the Boundary with Queenhithe Ward, is shown on Lambeth Hill, next to the *Green Dragon*, to the north of Thames Street. The lease had less than 30 years to run. St Andrew's church and Puddle Dock, where the Company had property, are marked at the western end of Thames Street. Everything shown here had been rebuilt since the Great Fire of 1666.

BY KIND PERMISSION OF THE GUILDHALL ART GALLERY, CITY OF LONDON

Rebuilding the Hall

On 2 December 1667 the Wardens began discussions with workmen about the rebuilding of their Hall. Until the new building was finished, the Wardens met at various inns: The Queen's Head, The Cock in Bishopgate, The Pope's Head, The Black Horse, and The White Lion; occasionally at the Old Bailey or the Guildhall; and sometimes beyond the City Walls in Southwark, Holborn or Westminster. The accounts for 1667–68 record: 'Spent attending the Committee for the City Lands and when the new lease was taken … Spent on several views of the Hall grounds … Paid for the Company's new lease of the ground on Lambeth Hill where the Hall and the two tenements formerly stood.' The same accounts record, 'Paid for a chest with three locks and a till in it with a Cock, wherein to put the plate, money and writings, £7 5s. 0d.' This is the Blacksmiths' Chest, now restored, which is kept in the hall of the Painter-Stainers' Company.

The Company had to borrow heavily in order to rebuild their Hall. The accounts for 1669–71 show that the carpenter was paid £450, the bricklayer £380, and other tradesmen £51 4s. 4d. The following year, another £366 was paid to the carpenter, £100 to the plasterer, and small sums to other craftsmen. The Hall was provided with a sundial and topped with a vane. The final payment for the Quest House was made in 1670, when the Company moved in to their new Hall. Mr Henry West, the Upper Warden, then returned the chest containing the Company's records and valuables, which had been in his safe custody. One of the Company's decisions was that the new Hall should contain a forge where former apprentices made their masterpieces to submit for approval before they could become freemen of the Company. In 1673–74 a carpenter was paid £36 2s. 0d. for building part of it and the rooms above, and another £31 10s. 0d. was spent on 'smiths' work upon building the Hall'.

Meanwhile, the Company rebuilt The Queen's Head and adjoining properties on St Andrew's Hill, near Puddle Wharf, but The Crown and Hoop and the blacksmith's shop by the Old Bailey were replaced by six brick houses, with 'yards, backsides and other parcels of ground'. The new tenants were not prepared to pay the old rents. In 1672–73 the Company's receipts from all sources amounted to £391 11s. 8d., compared with £477 5s. 4d. in the year before the Fire. Less money was coming in at the very time that it was needed most. In 1675–76 the Company had to pay £220 1s. 6d., the cost of the principal and the interest on loans obtained from private individuals and from the Company of Gardeners. When work on Lambeth Hill was nearly finished in 1676–77, a carver was paid £4 5s. 0d. 'for the Arms of the Company with the mantle and crest over the street door entering the Hall'.

The Hall was completed just in time to appear on John Ogilby's map of 1676, which showed that London was once again packed with buildings within its medieval street pattern. The City's physical appearance was now radically different, however, for the authorities had insisted that all new buildings should

Detail of Ogilby and Morgan's 1676 map, showing the maze of streets around St Andrew's church and Puddle Dock, where the Blacksmiths' Company had property.
© THE BRITISH LIBRARY BOARD, MAPS, CRACE II, 61

be constructed of brick. The second Blacksmiths' Hall must have looked very different from the old one, although it occupied the same plot.

An inventory of the charters, writings, plate, ornaments, goods, utensils, implements, and other things 'of and belonging to the Worshipful the Keepers or Wardens and Society of the Art and Mystery of the Blacksmiths, London, remaining in the Common Hall of the Society' was made in 1701. It provides a detailed picture of how the new Hall was furnished. The appraisers began by listing the silver plate: two dozen of spoons, one dozen of small wine cups, three tankards, six bowls; four large bowls with covers and a small, two-handled cup with a cover, known as a caudle cup, all gilt; five gilt salts, 'to wit, two double ones with tops, and one single one with a monument';

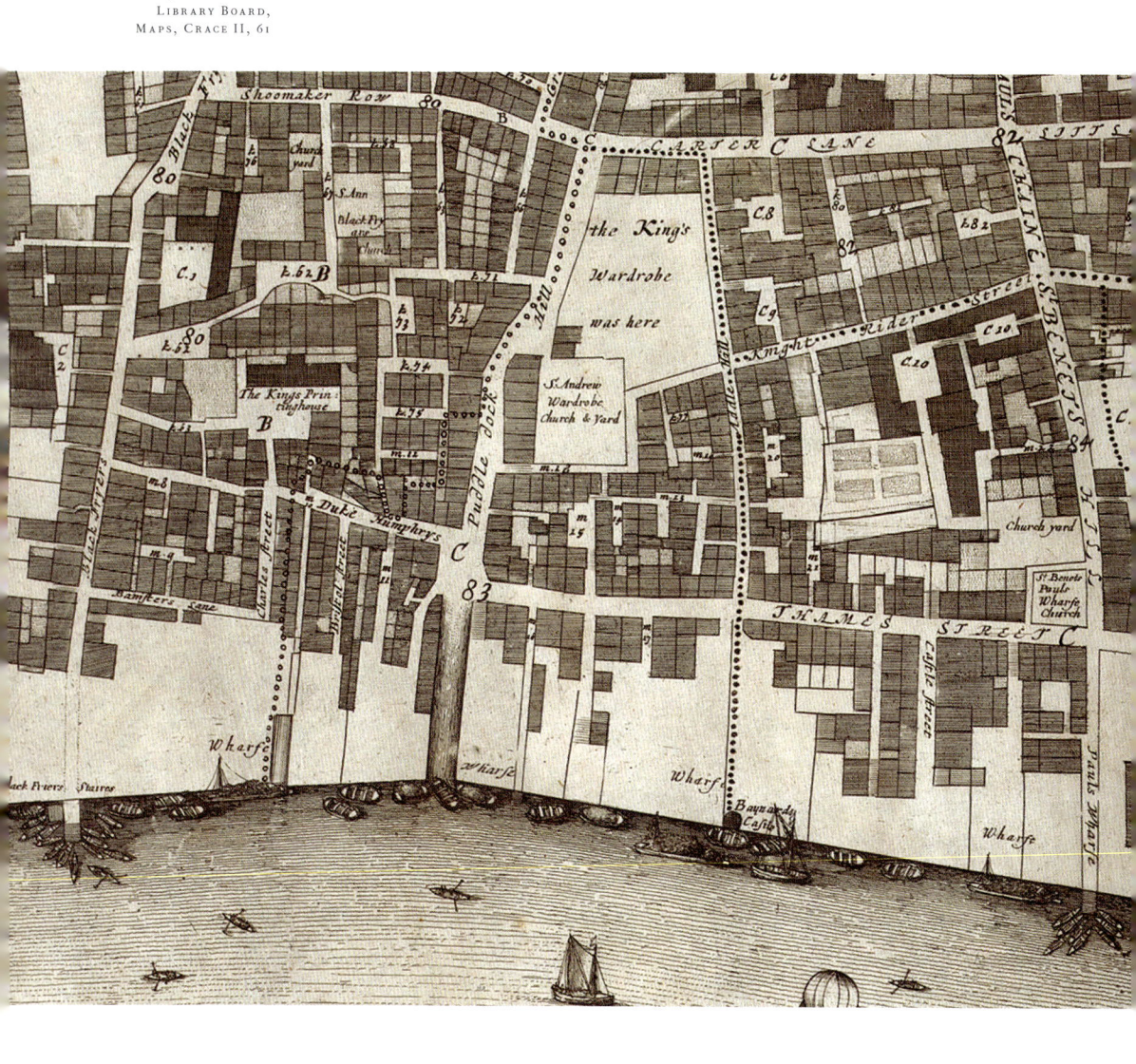

one anvil salt, and a gilt salt with a pyramid; three wooden bowls edged with silver gilt (which must have been the masers mentioned in earlier accounts); four law rolls of velvet crimson; a small iron box; the Poor's Box and an ivory hammer tipped with silver.

The parlour or court room contained an oval table, seven linen table cloths and five diaper napkins, a Turkey-work carpet, an elbow chair covered with crimson damask (the seat of the Upper Warden at the head of the table), 24 Turkey-work chairs (for the other Wardens and Assistants), cushions, some white figures, a pendulum clock, The King's Arms, a mantelpiece painted with pictures depicting the smith's craft, shovel and tongs, a pair of fire-dogs, corner irons, and an iron chimney back. Here, in this special room were kept a large Bible and 'The Vellum Book, wherein the Charter and Ordinances are inserted'.

In the lobby through the main entrance, a room which in the Old Hall had been known as the armoury, were two tables with old green-baize cloths, a pike, a musket, a pair of bandoleers, a belt, two swords, two carbines, and two pair of pistols with holsters. The room was adorned with the City's and Company's Arms, 'some figures of smithery, carved and painted', and several prints in black frames.

The central hall was furnished rather sparsely with three long tables and forms. The walls were decorated with three pictures, two 'gilded frames to some memorable transactions', the carved arms of Queen Elizabeth I, the painted Arms of King William III, and with the banners that were used on special occasions 'with the poles and hooks thereto belonging'.

The pewter room was well stocked with 58 dishes, 62 plates, 14 pie dishes, two pasty plates, seven pewter flagons, two copper flagons, a dozen pint pots, seven salts, 20 spoons, four dozen (new and old) black hafted knives and forks and six old white hafted forks and knives, four pair of brass candlesticks, four oval tin sconces, and 17 ordinary ones, four baskets and voiders, and a large chamber pot. The kitchen contained a leaded cistern and its appurtenances, a copper pot and cover, a brass copper, five trevets (three-footed metal stands placed over or before the fire), three iron dripping pans, a pair of racks, nine spits, two shovels and a fork.

In the shop (described in earlier records as the forge) were a beck iron for forging rings or bends, an anvil, a pair of bellows and forge, two vices, a slice, a fire staff, and two pair of tongs. Finally, a rolling stone and two ladders stood in the yard.

The new Hall was used by the Company for over 100 years. We have no

This eighteenth-century copy of an engraving by Wenceslaus Hollar in 1667, which in turn was based on 'An Exact Surveigh' taken by John Leake, shows the extent of the destruction caused by the Great Fire of London in 1666. Only a few streets in the north-eastern part of the City escaped the flames. In the west, the Fire spread beyond the City walls. In this version of Hollar's map the sites of the parish churches are marked and numbered and some major buildings are identified by letters in an accompanying key, such as M for Baynard's Castle. When the City was rebuilt after the Fire, the ancient street plan was by and large preserved.

MUSEUM OF LONDON

pictures of it, although its ground-plan is outlined on some seventeenth- and eighteenth-century maps, most clearly on John Ogilby's *Survey of the City* (1676). In his *The History of London* (1739) William Maitland observed that Lambeth Hill was 'a place well built and inhabited by private housekeepers' and that 'Of this hill is Blacksmiths' Hall, a good handsome building'. The high cost of repairs in later times causes us to question this judgement, however.

Royal Demands

What were the Company's other concerns in the late seventeenth and early eighteenth centuries? The Blacksmiths' paid hearth tax on the chimneys in their hall but seem to have made no protest against the levying of the tax on their members' forges, as distinct from their domestic hearths. This seems strange in view of the fact that The Company of Cutlers in Hallamshire conducted a vigorous campaign over many years; one of the results of their protest was that the tax collectors made lists of the cutlers, nailmakers and smiths of various kinds who steadfastly refused to pay. At Ladyday 1672, for instance about 600 smithy hearths were recorded in South Yorkshire and North Derbyshire, particularly in the district around Sheffield known anciently as Hallamshire. Regrettably, we do not have a comparable list of smiths in the City of London and its suburbs at that time. This indifference to the well-organised provincial campaign suggests that the Blacksmiths' Company and the other London livery companies responsible for various branches of the metal trades were not the force they once were.

The London livery companies had an unprecedented fight on their hands when the Catholic monarch, King James II, came to the throne in 1685. In common with many other associations up and down the land, the Blacksmiths' Company immediately sought, and were granted, a new royal charter confirming their ancient rights. But the signs of the coming struggle were already plain to see. The charter contained two new significant clauses: one insisting that the Wardens, Assistants and Clerk had to have received the Sacrament of the Church of England within six months before their election; and the other excluding Dissenters from their ranks. The Dissenters, or Nonconformists, were those people who had refused to conform to the Church of England as set out in a series of Acts passed in the years immediately after the Restoration of King Charles II in 1660. These Dissenters were the old Puritans who had been so influential in the livery companies before the Civil War and their successors. Collectively, they formed a resolute opposition to the new monarch's ambition to restore the Catholic Church as the state religion.

King James II took a firm line with those Dissenters who were in the upper ranks of their various livery companies. On 25 September 1687 he ordered the removal of the Wardens and eleven of the Assistants of the Blacksmiths' Company, that is about half the membership of the Court. Then, on 11 October 1687 he excluded another 37 livery men from the Company. We have only his orders and the laconic entries in the Company's minutes to inform us of these events, but clearly the impact was enormous. On 3 November 1687 nine new Assistants were chosen by the Blacksmiths, but five of these refused to take any other oaths except those of Allegiance and Supremacy, together with the Company's normal oath for Assistants. Despite the removal of leading figures, the Dissenting interest within the Company remained strong. This dispute rumbled on, with the removal of a further ten liverymen in February 1688, but a turning point in the larger struggle came in June that year when the seven bishops who had been imprisoned in the Tower of London for seditious libel were acquitted by a court of law. Before the year was out, King James had been forced to abdicate and William and Mary had been installed as joint rulers in his place. The London livery companies recovered their independence, the Dissenters gained freedom of worship, and the political crisis was over.

The Blacksmith's Trade

Shortly afterwards, a rare account of the working practices of the City's blacksmiths and other artisans is provided by the publication of Joseph Moxon's *Mechanick Exercises* (1694). This comprehensive guide to the great variety of crafts in London towards the close of the seventeenth century began with a 62-page account of smithing, accompanied by illustrations of a hearth, bellows, cooling trough, mould, work bench, and an anvil on a wooden block; also tools, including tongs, hammers, vices, screw plates, drills, files and rivets; and products such as hinges, locks, keys, bolts, nuts, and plates. The typical hearth was built of brick between 2 feet 6 inches and 2 feet 9 inches high and was connected to the bellows by a 'tewel pipe' to take the blast, and covered by a hovel that directed the smoke into a chimney. A blacksmith did not need much capital investment to set up in his trade, but the most successful required great technical skills. The standard of wrought ironwork was very high at the turn of the century and in the following decades, for this was the era of Jean Tijou at Hampton Court Palace and leading provincial craftsmen, led by Robert Bakewell of Derby, who specialised in gates, screens and arbours for houses, gardens and churches. The opportunities for skilled craftsmen were greater than ever before. On 29 October 1703 the Court of Assistants of the Blacksmiths' Company benefited from the 'extraordinary workmanship' of Nicholas Turner who presented them with a steel hammer, that is now kept at the Guildhall Museum. In return, he was admitted to the livery and given a gown.

Joseph Moxon reckoned that the iron that came from the Forest of Dean was of good quality, but other English iron was 'generally a coarse sort … hard and brittle, fit for fire-bars and other such coarse causes'. The highest-quality iron that was available to English blacksmiths came from Sweden. This was 'a fine, tough sort of iron' that would 'best endure the hammer and is softest to file' and so was 'much coveted'. Spanish iron was nearly as good and was particularly useful for welding, but it was liable to crack in the cooling process. German iron, however, was thought to be 'a bad coarse iron'. For tools, files and punches that needed a sharp cutting edge, the blacksmith, like the cutler, turned to cementation steel, which 'will work well at the forge and take a good heat', when it was sandwiched between two pieces of iron. In England, the Forest of Dean led the way in the manufacture of this type of steel, but Moxon also mentioned furnaces in Yorkshire, Gloucestershire, Sussex and the Weald of Kent. Foreign steel had long been imported, for the cementation furnace had been invented in Central Europe in the mid sixteenth century. 'Flemish' or 'German' steel was shipped down the Rhine from Cologne; Spanish steel was brought from the Basque Country across the Bay of Biscay; Swedish steel was transported via the Baltic and North Seas by merchants from Danzig; and Venice steel that made the long journey across the Mediterranean Sea and through the Straits of Gibraltar was used for small, sharp tools such as gravers, but also for razors and for surgical instruments.

Half a century later, R. Campbell published *The London Tradesman* (1747), which offered advice to fathers who were thinking of apprenticing a son to one of the trades or crafts in the capital city. The workmen in a smith's forge, he wrote, were divided into three classes: 'the Fire-man, or he that forges the work; the Vice-Man, or he who files and finishes it; and the Hammer-Man, who strikes with the great hammer by the direction of the Fire-Man, who uses only a small hammer'. Here we see the typical combination of a master and a couple of journeymen or apprentices. The lusty fellow who wielded the great hammer had the most laborious job but the smallest wage. He rarely received more than nine shillings a week, but in exceptional cases this might

Barge Banner. The date of this banner is not known, but is perhaps mid nineteenth century. It would have been flown when the Company hired a barge to follow the Lord Mayor on the Thames on his way to swear allegiance to the monarch. It is stored on a roll in special cloth at the Museum of London. A full-size replica was made for the Company's Float in the Lord Mayor's Show in 2005.

rise to twelve shillings. The Fire-Man was a skilled worker, who 'requires the greatest judgement, because taking the proper heats and forging the work is the most difficult part of the business'. The Vice-Man was just as important to the business, sometimes more so. Campbell thought that he 'requires the nicest hand and most mechanic head, especially if concerned in movements; and in such shops where works of that kind are chiefly carried on, he has the highest wages; but in shops where large and coarse works are performed the Fire-man earns most'.

Campbell was critical of the metalworker's reliance on the judgement of his eye. He concluded that 'smiths of all kind would be better workmen if they understood drawing so much as to plan their own works'. He acknowledged that 'all smiths require strength of body and a sound constitution to bear the labour and the heats and colds they are obliged to work through … They who work upon what appear to be trifling works require as much strength as those who are employed in heavier subjects.' As for apprentices, he thought that the heavy work involved meant that 'a boy can be of no service to any of the classes of smiths till he is about fifteen years of age'. He advised the learning of writing and arithmetic before a boy was bound to a master, 'for after he has begun to handle the hammer it is to no purpose to attempt to teach him the use of so small an instrument as that of a pen'. As with all crafts, the working day was long, generally from 6 o'clock in the morning to 8 o'clock at night, though these were not hours of incessant toil and workers had more leisure time than might be supposed, ranging from informal breaks to the celebration of numerous holy days.

Campbell also provides insights into special aspects of the blacksmith's trade. He tells us, for instance, that anvils were mostly made of iron but their face was of hardened steel. He observed that, 'The whole secret of the business consists of a just knowledge of tempering the steel'. The manufacture of anvils was 'abundantly profitable to the master', but the journeymen were paid no better than those doing common smiths' work. File making was another branch of the smith's craft which depended 'chiefly upon the secret of tempering, a thing never to be learned but by experience'. A file maker could earn from nine to fifteen shillings a week.

The range of the blacksmith's products and those of the brazier can be judged by what Campbell had to say about ironmongers' shops:

> in them you find grates and stoves of all fashions, pokers, fire shovels, tongs, and fenders, of polished iron, steel or brass: ranges for the

kitchen, jacks, spits, etc., coppers, kettles, fire pans, stew pans, of all sorts and sizes; candlesticks, snuffers, smoothing irons, box irons, and heaters; locks of all sorts, hinges of various kinds and different materials; chafes and handles for cabinet work, nails, wood screws, and generally all sorts of brass and iron work that are useful for furniture or any part of furniture.

The ironmonger was merely the middle man who supplied these goods to the public. Campbell wrote that, 'He employs the several classes of workmen, who apply themselves to the particular articles he wants, and his profit arises from the difference between the buying and selling prices'. The Ironmongers, of course, had their own livery company, an ancient institution that ranks tenth amongst the 'Great Twelve'. The Blacksmiths' Company apparently had nothing to do with them at that time.

Declining Powers

The building of the Blacksmiths' new Hall after the Fire came at a time when livery company control of London's crafts and retail trades was beginning to wane. Even before the Civil War, the huge growth of the population of the City and its suburbs meant that the Corporation and the livery companies were unable to curb retail sales of goods by 'foreigners' who were not members of any company. Nor could they insist that a seven-year apprenticeship leading to a freedom was the only way into a trade. The Fire drove even more people beyond the City Walls into the suburbs, where it was difficult to enforce regulations. When houses and workshops were rebuilt and craftsmen set up business again, the Corporation and the livery companies had little choice other than to be more liberal towards resident 'foreigners'. From 1672 they were no longer prosecuted, and from the following year anyone who took up permanent residence in the newly built houses and shops were admitted into the freedom of the City without charge or qualification. Between 1675 and 1680 the total number of freemen's admissions within the City rose to over 10,000. Most of these new freemen were small shopkeepers and craftsmen and they included large numbers of 'foreigners'. The Corporation was no longer in charge of the way that London's trade was conducted.

By the early eighteenth century the legality of livery company rights to control trade was increasingly challenged at law, even though these rights were enshrined in royal charters. The spirit of the new age was to cast aside old

Carved ivory hammer with silver mounts, engraved with the Company's Motto and seal. It dates from about 1700.

restrictions and to allow the unfettered expansion of trade. The most important power that a company possessed was the right to search, an essential privilege if companies were to regulate their trades and maintain their monopolies. The growth of London beyond its ancient limits had long made such a right difficult to enforce in Westminster and the suburbs. By the end of the seventeenth century, doubts about the legality of searches meant that, even in the City, companies were increasingly reluctant to act for fear of prosecution for trespass.

Five legal cases challenged these ancient rights, but the livery companies hung on as best they could. The only clue about the Blacksmiths' concerns at this time is provided by a minute of the Wardens' Court held on 24 June 1712: 'At this Court great part of the Bye Laws were read'. During the following month, the Corporation tried again to enforce the ancient rule that a grant of the freedom of the City was necessary before any Londoner was allowed to practise a craft. For a while, this new resolution encouraged many livery companies to carry out searches and to collect Quarterage with renewed vigour, but the time, trouble and expense that this involved soon brought a harsh dose of reality. Soon, searches were carried out reluctantly or perfunctorily. From the craftsman's point of view, the economic benefits of gaining admission to the freedom of a London company had become far less apparent than in earlier times. The ready market for their goods encouraged them to go their own ways. In an expanding economy, they no longer sought the protection of an association whose main purpose was to restrict trade so that their members' jobs and wage levels were secure. Most of London's livery companies were faced with the same problems in a difficult period of transition in the first half of the eighteenth century. Looking back, it is perhaps surprising that they tried so hard to maintain their ancient rights, for so long.

In companies such as the Blacksmiths, the skilled workers who adapted their work to meet the changing demands of fashion, saw the need to reject the old restrictions. In 1716, for instance, the City's Court of Aldermen heard complaints from William Harding, a free blacksmith, who had been refused permission by the Blacksmiths' Company, because of the 1712 Act, to employ 'foreigners', although 'he could not get freemen to do his work, being engine work of new invention'. But fewer freemen meant a loss of revenue for the Company. On 1 July 1714 the Blacksmiths resolved to let their Hall for occasional use, at the discretion of the Wardens.

Apprentices

As the eighteenth century progressed, fewer boys sought a formal apprenticeship in the London crafts and retail trades. The advantages of securing a freedom through serving an apprenticeship lessened once membership of a livery company became increasingly open to purchase and, as the capital city expanded, a large amount of business was conducted well beyond its medieval walls. Membership of a livery company was no longer a sure indication of a man's occupation, especially for the prestigious 'Great Twelve'. By the early eighteenth century many companies had such a mixed membership that loyalty to a craft or occupation must have diminished. Nevertheless, most Londoners who earned their living from business still belonged to a livery company, even though membership declined from a peak figure of over 2,000 new freemen in the City in the late 1670s, when entry restrictions were temporarily relaxed, to 1,250 a year in the 1740s. Stark as they are, these absolute figures do not reveal how far membership had declined relative to London's rising population.

Even those who followed the ancient method of entering a trade through apprenticeship often took no active interest in their livery company once they had earned their freedom. Those young men who wished to earn a decent living as a master, however, had no choice but to move up a step by joining the 'clothing' or livery. By the late seventeenth century, most of the City's companies had realised that the easiest way to raise money for their activities was to increase the number of liverymen and to charge high entry fines; freemen who refused to comply were threatened with prosecution, and only a minority of those who pleaded to be excused were successful. Liverymen attended company dinners and processions, when they wore the livery gown, but they had no duties other than to elect the Wardens and Assistants from their ranks.

The Blacksmiths responded to these problems in similar ways to the other livery companies, with much wrangling amongst the membership on how best to proceed. The Company's authority was being questioned, but litigation cost a lot of money, which was difficult to raise. The Blacksmiths' Company was nevertheless persistent in prosecuting and charging people with various offences against its charters and ordinances. It was not until the last quarter of the eighteenth century that the Wardens and Assistants reluctantly abandoned their power of search and their insistence on the payment of quarterly subscriptions.

For much of the eighteenth century, the apprenticeship system continued to function as before for many of the boys who wished to enter the blacksmith's trade. The Company's five volumes of apprentice bindings registered boys up to 1781. The 'Blacksmiths' Orphans' Book, 1694–1747' shows that large numbers of poor boys who had lost their parents were apprenticed upon receipt of a premium paid for by the overseer of the poor of his parish. In the year beginning 15 December 1694 the 'bindings of poor apprentices' amounted to 101, at an average premium of £6 12s. 6d. The following year 134 poor boys were bound, and similar numbers entered the trade in succeeding years. They were generally welcomed by small masters who were thankful for the premium and pleased to have an extra worker in return for the cost of maintaining him.

The 'Apprentices Turnover Book', covering the period 1702–70, provides many examples of another feature of the old system that arose when a master died or when it was agreed that perhaps the boy had no aptitude for the craft and wanted to try something else. Three examples from 7 May 1702 illustrate the usual types of entry:

> John Phillips put apprentice to John Hall, afterwards turned over to James Penny, now turned over to John Carter.
>
> George Wood put apprentice to Richard Liddiard, deceased, with the consent of Elizabeth his relict, executor, turned over to Mark Liddiard.
>
> William Crouch put apprentice to Samuel Smell having been discharged by the Chamberlain turned over to Richard Bell, longbow string maker.

Other apprentice boys at this time were turned over not only to other blacksmiths but to men with such varied occupations as merchant tailor, clothworker, saddler, stationer, vintner, cordwainer, bricklayer, and basket maker. A most unusual entry for 25 August 1699 recorded that an apprentice of a deceased master was turned over to 'Mary Wood of this Company and Art'. Was she perhaps the widow of a blacksmith who was allowed to continue to supervise his trade?

Disputes and Challenges

A long-running legal dispute with the Clockmakers' Company began in 1697. The Clockmakers had acquired a charter in 1631 and now they wanted full control over their trade, including the manufacture of 'clocks, watches, alarums, boxes or cases of such, mathematical instruments, dialling, and other work'. But they were a small company with no liverymen, and they were unable to match the strength of the Blacksmiths, who argued that it was well known that they were 'the original and proper makers of Clocks, etc.', that their members had 'full skill and knowledge therein', and that 'many of their employments are wholly in such work'. The Clockmakers were defeated on this occasion and had to wait until 1765 before they were successful.

Another group whose activities concerned the Blacksmiths' Company were the unlicensed hawkers and pedlars who sold imported wares. A tract published in London in 1691 claimed that pedlars and hawkers had multiplied daily and within the last few years had trebled in number, but when the House of Commons debated the matter that year the convenience and cheapness of having goods brought to the door won the day and the motion to suppress hawkers and pedlars was lost. Nine years later, however, the Blacksmiths' Company was still concerned about this infringement of their charter. The accounts for 4 January 1700 show them proposing more effectual methods for suppressing hawkers. On 23 January four liverymen were appointed for this task, but they were fighting a losing battle.

The Company's records also reveal tensions between various members, particularly in 1700 when the Upper Warden, Mr Markham, was suspended after irregularities had been discovered in his accounts. He was charged with wasting the Company's money and wronging them in false charges. Markham was ejected from office, but was eventually reinstated in the Court. It seems that his accounts were in a muddle not because of dishonesty but through careless neglect. At that time, the four chief officers of the Company were referred to in the minutes as Upper Warden, Second Warden, Guildhall Warden, and Renter Warden. Later in the century, the Wardens were ranked as Upper, Renter, House, and Guildhall.

The Company had long been concerned with 'foreigners' and had instigated many prosecutions, but on 22 May 1701 the impossibility of enforcing the law upon so many offenders was recognised reluctantly. The 'foreigners' were accepted as 'Brethren of the Art and Mystery of Smithery' and were allowed to have their own organisation within the Company. The resolution reads:

> And for that all Smiths living within four miles of the said City, of which there is yet a great number not admitted into this Company, ought to be members of this Company, and they to bind their apprentices, to pay Quarterage, and to be conformable and subject to all the wholesome and good Bye-laws and Ordinances of the said Company.

Henceforth, the Blacksmiths' records speak of 'The Foreign Members or Sworn Brothers of the same Company'.

The difficulties that the Company faced are also obvious from the challenges that were made to their power of search. On 4 September 1701 the accounts noted that the searches made the previous August had resulted in a confrontation with a Mr Wire, a Tire-smith of Kingsland Street beyond Shoreditch, who had refused to pay the duty. During the same search, a Mr Adams, described as 'a vendor of new as well as old iron and other wares, in the High Street, Shoreditch', had opposed the search and had 'abused and reviled the Wardens'. He had been taken before a Justice of the Peace, who had reprimanded him severely, but the Upper Warden of the Company declared his willingness 'to avoid all rigour and severity', and offered Adams better terms than those mentioned by the JP, whereupon Adams agreed. The Wardens were weakening in their resolve.

Tensions between the Wardens and Assistants on the one hand and members of the Livery on the other surfaced in the first decade of the eighteenth century, when a group of liverymen petitioned the Lord Mayor to be allowed to see their own charters and bye-laws. These liverymen claimed that they were excluded from decision making by a self-

Silver porringer made in London in 1704 and donated by a couple known only by their initials (M & M L). It was sold after the Blacksmiths' Hall was abandoned, but was purchased and restored to the Company in 1897 by Alex Frazer, Father of the Company.

electing elite, whose exorbitant fines and extravagant eating and drinking had run the Company into debt. The Wardens and Assistants refused to meet the liverymen to discuss the charters and bye-laws and tried to evade the ruling of the Mayor's Court until they began to quarrel amongst themselves and the Upper Warden resigned in exasperation. This was a foretaste of what was to come. The frequent summoning of members to pay Quarterage led the Beadle to ask that an Under-Beadle be appointed to assist him (as in the previous century), and in 1732 William Plivey was appointed to this new post.

The Final Years of the Old Company

On 7 April 1743 the Company decided to start proceedings to renew the lease of the Hall and to dispose of their South Sea Annuity Stock to pay for it. On 12 January 1744 they rejected the terms that were offered by the City authorities, but in September of that year they agreed to pay £300 to take a new lease of their Hall for 40 years, once the old one expired. This was paid in the following month, but four years later the Company had long discussions on the high cost of the lease and the need to spend heavily upon the Hall's repair. This became a problem that would not go away. Yet the Company's minutes record the unchanging pattern of meetings and special events that continued despite all these concerns. On 27 June 1750, for example, it was: 'Ordered that Notice be given to the Livery by an Advertisement in the Daily Advertizer to appear at Guildhall in their Livery Gowns' for the election of a sheriff. But, unsurprisingly, it was becoming increasingly difficult to persuade liverymen to accept office. The Wardens' role had become more demanding and more expensive. The Company's accounts note numerous requests for the postponement of a stewardship and the regular levying of fines on those who declined to serve. The number of liverymen in the Blacksmiths' Company rose from 176 in 1699 to 225 in 1724 as the Company tried to increase its revenue, but we do not know the size of the Yeomanry or of

Silver brandy warmer with turned wood handle, made in London in 1736.

the Foreign Brethren. The accounts for 1731–32 show that the income of the Company was largely derived from fines and fees, but that the collection of these payments was proving difficult. In contrast to earlier times, rents now comprised a small part of annual income. A welcome source of revenue came from the Plantations in Northern Ireland that King James I had forced the London livery companies to finance; in 1750, for instance, 'The Renter Warden with the Clerk attended at Vintners Hall and received the Company's dividend of the Irish Rents, £27 5s. 6d.'

Recruitment to the City livery companies declined steadily in the second and third decades of the eighteenth century. Efforts were made to buck this trend. Between 1750 and 1778 no fewer than 22 livery companies, including the Blacksmiths, obtained Acts of Common Council which reaffirmed their right to compel those who practised their trade to join their ranks. The Company's minutes record that in 1752 the Blacksmiths petitioned the Clerk of the Crown in Chancery for a confirmation of their bye-laws. But such efforts were in vain. The average number of freemen who were admitted to the Blacksmiths' Company during the previous five years was 17; during the next five years it rose only slightly to 18, despite the continued rise in the population. Other minutes provide brief glimpses of the arguments that raged again within the Wardens' courts. On 5 April 1753 it was agreed that 'the Charter be publicly read on the 10th at 2 p.m. in the Hall', but when 'the dissatisfied Livery attended on notice to hear the Charter read' they 'departed seemingly satisfied without making any further requests'.

The Minute Book for 1779–85 is the main source of evidence for the critical years leading up to the decision to abandon the lease of the Hall. The minutes provide numerous examples of the Company's last efforts to enforce their authority and to insist on the continuation of past procedures. On 5 August 1779, for instance, an order was placed on James Pilgrim, who had refused 'to pay his Yeomanry fine and come on the livery', but as he had already been 'summoned several times and did not attend', it seemed unlikely that he would comply. The most original excuse for not being a freeman of the Company was offered in 1780 by Henry Townes, who claimed that 'he was entitled to carry on the Trade of a Smith by serving His Majesty in the rebellion of 1745'. Some of those who were summonsed eventually paid up, but the Company faced a losing battle.

On 27 July 1780 John Horton, the Upper Warden, seconded by another Warden, moved that because of 'the very great expense incurred by keeping the Hall for doing the Company's business' that 'the Hall be advertized to be let for the remainder of the term in the Company's lease'. This was agreed, though one of the Assistants, Clement Meymott, was suspended 'for abusing Mr Horton on the last Quarterly Court'. On 3 January 1782 Meymott was discharged from the Court of Assistants 'on account of his ill behaviour at the different courts of the Company as also to the several members thereof'. This motion was carried unanimously, so it seems that Meymott was alone in not accepting the critical situation in which the Company found itself.

The impotence of the Company in defending its members' interests is revealed by the reaction to the petition of Seth Smith, liveryman, which was debated on 18 January 1781. Smith lived in Queen Street, Cheapside, next door to an attorney, who had taken an action at law complaining that the noises made in the workshop were a nuisance. The court upheld Smith's right to follow his trade, but the attorney also complained that the chimney from Smith's forge was only about seven feet from his stair case window. The three City surveyors who were called to the site judged that the chimney did not obstruct the light, but four members of the jury that examined the case said that the light was obstructed to a very small degree and so awarded the attorney five shillings damages. This meant, however, that Smith was liable for the full costs of the case. He pulled down his chimney but was unable to pay the legal costs and faced 'utter ruin' by the threat of another action, unless the Company came to his aid. The Company felt unable to offer any support, though twelve Wardens and assistants personally contributed a guinea each to Smith's cause.

Outwardly, everything carried on as normal. In 1781 a new Clerk was chosen, and although the Company's apprenticeship binding books end that year, new apprentices were still recorded in the minutes. Now, however, the majority of boys came from London and its suburbs instead of distant parts of the country. But more signs of the growing financial crisis appear in the minutes for the following year. On 16 May 1782 it was agreed that the hall and committee room (once known as the parlour) should be rented to the master and scholars of St Paul's School at the yearly rent of £30. On 4 July the Company dispensed with the services of an Under Beadle, whose tasks were now included with those of the Beadle, and on the same day, a survey was made of the Company's estates. In an attempt to increase the revenue from subscriptions, it was agreed on 3 July 1783 that a person should be appointed 'to collect the Quarterage due at Midsummer last and that he be allowed for collecting the same ten per cent and that he take an account of all persons following the trade of a smith within the limits of the Company's

Tankards. Plain quart bellied tankards with thread waists, made in London in 1752 (*left*; donated by S. Need) and 1748 (*right*) and inscribed with the Company's Arms.

Pint mugs made in London in (*from left*) 1754, 1766 and 1765, the last two engraved with the Company's Arms.

bye-laws not being free of the Company'. Smiths from all parts of the country who had settled in and around the City of London refused to pay quarterly subscriptions or to conform to the Blacksmiths' charter and bye-laws. The huge rise in the national population in the late eighteenth century meant that it was physically impossible to control any of London's trades and crafts in the old manner. By 1801, when the first national census was taken, London's population had rocketed to about 959,300.

Inserted in the minutes for 26 September 1783 is a lengthy case concerning the Company's right to enforce the payment of fines and Quarterage. The Counsel's opinion was that, as the Company's charters had never been tested at law, there was no guide to usage. The Company would have to rely upon the words of the charters, but he warned that the 'Courts of Justice will incline against every restriction of trade'. No precise sum of Quarterage was mentioned in the charters, so any attempt to enforce payment would best be done by 'an action of debt for the sum ascertained in the Bye Law'. He suggested that, as the charter of King James II had never been acted under, the legality of the charter of King Charles I should be the one to be tested in court. He advised careful use of the power of seizure, for (unlike the power of other City companies) this had not been confirmed by Act of Parliament. The Company, wisely, never went to the expense of a trial by law.

Unable to enforce their ancient authority, the Wardens and Assistants called a meeting of their Court on 28 May 1784 to consider what to do about the bad state of the Hall. It was agreed unanimously that, considering the short term of the remainder of the lease, no repairs would be carried out other than those that were judged necessary to keep the premises in 'tenantable repair'. Minds were concentrated as the end of the lease drew near. On 7 October that year, it was agreed that, because of the great expense incurred by keeping the Hall for doing the Company's business, the City authorities should be approached to seek release from the remaining four years of the lease. A month later, however, 120 liverymen still met for their annual dinner, though on this occasion they forsook their Hall and asked Mr Marriott of Paul's Head Tavern, Cateaton Street, to provide a meal at 4*s*. 6*d*. per head.

The dinner was perhaps not as convivial as usual. On 7 April 1785 the Mayor and Aldermen accepted the surrender of the lease of the Hall at the following Michaelmas (29 September). On 16 June the Company's silver plate was offered for sale and the money was laid out in the purchase of 3 per cent Consolidated Bank Annuities so that the interest arising therefrom could be paid to the poor of the Company. The deal was completed on 14 October 1785 at the Rainbow Coffee House in Cornhill. Since that date, the Company has maintained its ancient customs and traditions and its funds have been devoted to charitable and educational purposes and to the encouragement of the trade, but it has not had a Hall of its own.

The City Corporation let the former hall as a warehouse. In 1794 a *Dictionary of London and Westminster, and Borough of Southwark* noted that T. J. & R. Pidcock occupied a Bottle Warehouse at 23 Lambeth Hill and that the premises of R. Buchanan & Co., Wine & Brandy Merchants, were at the same address. In 1831 James Elmes, *A Topographical Dictionary of London and Its Environs* stated that the ancient hall had gone to decay and was let as a warehouse. According to other publications, it was still being used as a warehouse in 1878 and 1892.

Despite the loss of their Hall and the valuables that adorned it, the Wardens and Assistants continued to accept apprentices to the trade, to summon freemen to join the Livery, and to fine those who refused to accept office, such as that of steward on procession days. They attempted to run the Company's affairs as before and they re-elected the Clerk and the Beadle. That November, Mr Samuel Marriott was again asked to provide a dinner for 120 of the Livery, on slightly reduced terms. He was allowed 'four shillings per head (including strong beer, ale, bread, beer, cheese, lemons, etc.) and ten shillings for the glass broke on that day'. Meanwhile, the Wardens also used The Horns, Kennington, and The Queen's Arms, St Paul's Churchyard, for their business meetings, but in 1786 it was resolved that the courts be held at the George and Vulture Tavern in Cornhill. The Company had returned to the district where they had started, five centuries previously.

Social activities went on as before, including the Lord Mayor's procession and annual Livery dinners, and although the Company of Blacksmiths had lost their Hall they had not yet given up the fight to restrict trade to their members. On 2 October 1788 the Clerk was ordered to prepare a case for the opinion of Counsel respecting persons carrying on the trade of blacksmith within the City or the limits of their charter who were not freemen of the Company. Internal dissension about the best way ahead continued, with the Wardens and Assistants being only a little more amenable than their predecessors to demands from the Livery. The minutes record that on 4 October 1792

> the petition of George Wapshott and others requesting to be permitted to inspect the Company's Charter and Bye-Laws (respecting persons following the trade of a Smith not having served an apprenticeship of seven years) was read and it was ordered that their attorney be permitted to inspect the Charter and Bye-Laws but not to take extracts or copies.

The Company's financial state had deteriorated a little more by 6 October 1796, when it was agreed that 'the ancient custom of paying the sum of one shilling to each member who attended the Quarterly Courts be omitted'. It was also resolved that the Wardens should not dine at the expense of the Company at the Monthly Courts. The Company lost revenue when it failed to make its freemen join the Livery. On 6 April 1797 it was ordered that the Clerk proceed at Law against the several persons who having been duly and regularly summoned to attend and take up the Livery and Freedom and disobeyed and neglected the Summons: and that every Member who refuses to pay be likewise proceeded against.

Few of those who were summoned took any notice, however. At the close of the eighteenth century the Company found itself in a worse position than ever before. Yet, somehow, when an appeal was made for 'a subscription now open at the Bank for the defence of the Country' at the time of the French Revolutionary Wars, the Blacksmiths' Company managed to contribute the handsome sum of £105. All was not yet lost.

Plaque marking the site of the Hall that was built after the Great Fire of London and which was sold by the Company in 1785. The earlier, medieval Hall had occupied the same site on Lambeth Hill.

4 Finding a New Role

THE RISE OF THE IRON INDUSTRY

In the first half of the eighteenth century Britain was generally short of iron, so much so that blacksmiths were often prepared to accept scrap iron in part payment for work done. But then came a series of technological breakthroughs, starting with coke smelting by the Darbys at Coalbrookdale in Shropshire. Once Henry Cort's methods of making strong and workable wrought iron in 'puddling furnaces' were widely adopted in the 1780s the progress of the national iron industry was rapid.

By the beginning of Queen Victoria's reign new types of furnaces, powered by steam, had doubled British output of pig iron. Large ironworks were flourishing in south Wales, Staffordshire, Derbyshire, Lancashire, Yorkshire, and central Scotland. The new companies commonly owned and worked coal and ironstone mines, coking plants, furnaces, foundries, rolling mills and associated departments. Before the great expansion of the steel industry in the second half of the nineteenth century, architects and civil engineers preferred wrought iron for its strength and its ability to resist shocks and corrosion. It was used not only for farm machinery and power looms in textile factories, but for the new railways and ocean-going steamships, notably Brunel's *Great Eastern* of 1858, and for major civil engineering projects, such as the great London bridges and the construction of the Crystal Palace. Victorian ironworks developed a wide range of machine tools which were sold around the world, and they made the stoves, fire ranges, fenders and pipes that did so much to improve the standard of comfort in homes throughout the land.

At the peak of the wrought iron industry in 1875 Britain had 314 ironworks, 7,575 furnaces, 909 rolling mills, and an annual production of about 4½ million tons. Thirty years later, however, production had fallen

Snuff box made in Birmingham in 1874 and engraved with the Company's Arms. It was presented to the Company by Lt Col. Robertson two years later.

to about one million tons per annum in face of competition from steel. The blast furnaces, puddling furnaces and rolling mills of the great ironworks had made Victorian Britain 'the workshop of the world'. Incredible quantities of tools and manufactured goods were exported from the metal-working districts of northern and midland England, Wales and Scotland to distant parts of the Empire. At the beginning of the twentieth century, the various metal industries provided employment for nearly one million British people.

THE TRADITIONAL BLACKSMITH

The greater availability of iron and improved transport reduced the blacksmith's costs. He became the dominant craftsman in the countryside as iron began to replace wood in even the remotest areas. The Board of Agriculture's county reports from the years after 1790 recorded numerous examples of creative local smiths, who designed new ploughs, machines and tools. But their products were manufactured only on a small, local scale. The output of the country smith was modest indeed when compared with that of the new foundries in the manufacturing towns.

The blacksmith's dependency upon his manual skills and experienced eye was no match for the new technology. The anvil and the hand hammer

Old Smithy, Lordship Place, Chelsea, drawn by William Walter Burgess in the late Victorian or Edwardian era. The local smithy was a ubiquitous feature within cities and towns as well as villages and rural areas.
MUSEUM OF LONDON

had been replaced by the hydraulic forging press of 4,000 or possibly 6,000 tons. Yet the craft of the blacksmith continued to flourish in town and countryside alike, for the growing number of horses needed to be shod. It has been estimated that in 1900 Britain had 3½ million horses, of which two million were directly employed in agriculture. Victorian London was still a horse-drawn society. At the end of the nineteenth century Greater London had nearly a quarter of a million horses pulling road vehicles of all kinds; some 80,000 of these horses powered the omnibuses and trams that brought people into work from the suburbs. Town horses had to go to the blacksmith's or farrier's forge every three or four weeks for re-shoeing, whereas country horses that worked chiefly on the land were brought in to be shod once every three months on average. The difference in timing was because town horses worked such long distances on the roads during a day that they got into the habit of sliding and dragging their feet, which burnt out their shoes.

Shoeing horses and making and repairing farm tools and machinery were the mainstays of the country blacksmith. He was not a specialist but a man who could turn his hand to any job that came along. At the time of the 1851 census about 94,000 blacksmiths were at work in England and Wales. Twenty years later the number had risen to about 112,000.

In his book *The Horse in the Furrow* George Ewart Evans recorded the memories of Suffolk blacksmiths who had worked in the first half of the twentieth century. One of his informants was Clifford Race, who had served an apprenticeship with a blacksmith at Creeting, but who worked for many years after the First World War at Needham Market, a large village near Ipswich:

> Nine of us worked at Day's the blacksmith's; two of us did nothing all day but shoeing. The day started at six in the morning and went on till six in the evening. The nine of us were put out to jobs like this: two were on the shoeing – two more were brought in if there was a rush; the guv'nor would be making mill bills – a tool for trimming a millstone; two were on farm-work, sharpening the tines of harrows, mending ploughs and so on; the last four were normally on outside jobs, on pumps for wells – outside work of all kinds. During the twelve-hour day the two of us aimed to do 36 shoes, that is nine horses. Two of us averaged four shoes an hour.

The smithy was not only a regular place of call for local farmers; it was where they could exchange news about horses and markets. Clifford Race recalled that sometimes eight or nine people would be standing about gossiping, getting in his way as he tried to do his job. Few people could judge what shape a horse was in better than the blacksmith who shod him. The farmers knew this and so they would drop in for advice when they were thinking of buying a horse. In the days before the professional vet, a skilled smith acted as a horse doctor.

The tools that the village blacksmiths made for farmers varied considerably in style from one district to another and they were often shaped to suit the requirements of individual workers, for this could mean real savings in labour during a day's work. Even in the early twentieth century village blacksmiths were willing to make a tool to order. In *Five Miles from Bunkum*, the local name for Saffron Walden, Charles Cooper, a blacksmith at Ashdon, recalled that:

> Farm workers came with problems, for most of the labourers had to find their own tools. They asked for left-handed scythes, wider

or narrower hoe blades to chop out weeds from wide or narrow drillings; men with big arms would demand longer scythe blades, and gamekeepers and poachers asked for long bladed curved spades to dig out rabbits and ferrets. [The blacksmith] sharpened bill-hooks, scythes, sickles, axes, and every type of edged tool, often replacing the broken or split staves and stales. He made pitchforks and four-tined forks, plough spuds, coulters, shears, drills and harrows; sometimes renewing the entire set of teeth on worn out harrows.

Many implements were made jointly by different village craftsmen, in particular the blacksmith, carpenter and wheelwright. The re-tyring of wooden cart wheels was a regular job for the rural smith because in the summer the woodwork in the farm cart or wagon wheels tended to shrink and the iron tyres often worked loose. Welding was another basic task and fire-welded repairs to farm machines became an important part of the blacksmith's work. In the Victorian era a local smith was often asked to make new parts and alterations to machines, and by the end of the nineteenth century he was turning his hand to repairing and maintaining bicycles. The work was skilled and hard, but small in scale; rural smithies generally employed no more than two to four men.

The Company

The Court Minute Books for the first quarter of the nineteenth century show that the Blacksmiths' Company was still occasionally binding apprentices, admitting liverymen, and paying its poorest members quarterly pensions. On paper, if not in reality, the whole system of guild privilege remained intact. Suddenly, and without any explanation, the minutes from the first Court meeting of 1800 start to refer to the leading figure in the company as the Prime Warden rather than the Upper Warden. Today, just six London livery companies do not have a Master: the Fishmongers, Goldsmiths, Dyers, Blacksmiths, and Basketmakers each have a Prime Warden, and the Weavers have an Upper Bailiff; while the Shipwrights have a permanent Master with an annually elected Prime Warden. In the early nineteenth century the Blacksmiths' Company minutes refer to the Prime, Renter, House, and Guildhall Wardens, but eventually the old titles of House and Guildhall Warden were replaced by the less colourful Third and Fourth Warden, again without explanation.

Renter Warden's badge. This 18 carat yellow gold badge with enamel Coat of Arms and Motto and white gold Knight's helmet, made in Birmingham, was presented by Alfred Barrow, the Father of the Company, in 1937.

Fourth Warden's badge. Alfred Barrow also presented this 18 carat yellow gold and black enamel badge with white gold Knight's helmet in 1937. It was made in Birmingham.

On 6 August 1812 the Court agreed to purchase 200 Consolidated Stocks 'in addition to the Company's present Stock of 1,700'. But the financial situation was worrying. On 7 October 1813 it was minuted that 'the resolution for having a Livery dinner in celebration of Lord Mayor's day be rescinded in consequence of a sufficient number of Stewards fines not having been collected to defray the expenses thereof'. On 4 July 1816 it was resolved

'That the Court Dine on the Election Day being 1 August at the Ship Tavern, Greenwich, at half past three o'clock precisely', but on 3 October 1816 a member's proposal for almshouses 'for the reception and maintenance of their decayed Liverymen' was defeated by a show of hands on the grounds that the Company had insufficient funds.

The members of the Court often found that they now had very little or no business. For example, on four occasions between 5 September 1839 and 5 May 1842 only four or five members attended the monthly meeting and no business was placed before them. On nine other occasions between September 1857 and March 1868 meetings were cancelled because of lack of business. The Company no longer had a real sense of purpose. By the mid nineteenth century the links between London's livery companies and the ancient crafts that they had represented since the Middle Ages had weakened considerably. The liverymen's principal concerns now were the administration of their freehold and trust estates and their convivial feasting. On 7 April 1853, for instance, the Court dined at the Plough Tavern, Blackwall. Soon, they would be going much further afield for their 'Summer Entertainments'.

The Blacksmiths were one of the poorer companies in the City. On 2 October 1856, for example, the Renter Warden reported an annual income of £433 9s. 3d. and an expenditure of £425 17s. 11d. The spending of £425 13s. 3½d. in 1859–60 against an income of only £375 16s. 3d. was very unusual. The Company was unable to support more than a few charities and on 4 October 1866 they agreed to reduce the list of their pensioners, both male and female, from 24 to 16.

Company properties

John Noorthouck, *A New History of London* (1773) had noted that 'The company of Blacksmiths have a neat hall situated on Lambeth hill', but as we have seen the Company relinquished the lease twelve years later. Long after the building was converted into a warehouse, its original function was remembered by commentators on the London scene. James Elmes, *A Topographical Dictionary of London and Its Environs* (1831) observed that the Blacksmiths' Company 'is governed by a master, three wardens, and twenty-one assistants. It is the fortieth in the city list. Since the company has relinquished the use of its hall on Lambeth-hill, the business is conducted at Cutlers-hall'. W. Thornbury, *Old & New London*, vol. 2 (1878) and C. Hazlitt, *The Livery Companies of the City of London* (Macmillan, 1892) both noted that the former Hall was still used as a warehouse. The area around the Hall was altered greatly between 1863 and 1871 when Queen Victoria Street was constructed to improve the approach to the central banking district. This new street was nearly two-thirds of a mile long and the scheme cost over £1 million. The numerous lanes, alleys and courts that were swept away included part of Lambeth Hill, but an Ordnance Survey map of 1873 shows that the warehouse which was once the Blacksmiths' Hall had survived. In 1881 the Salvation Army built their headquarters at 101 Queen Victoria Street, including parts of Lambeth Hill, Booth Lane and Peter's Hill. On 2 June 1932 the Court of the Blacksmiths' Company recorded in their minutes that the Salvation Army had

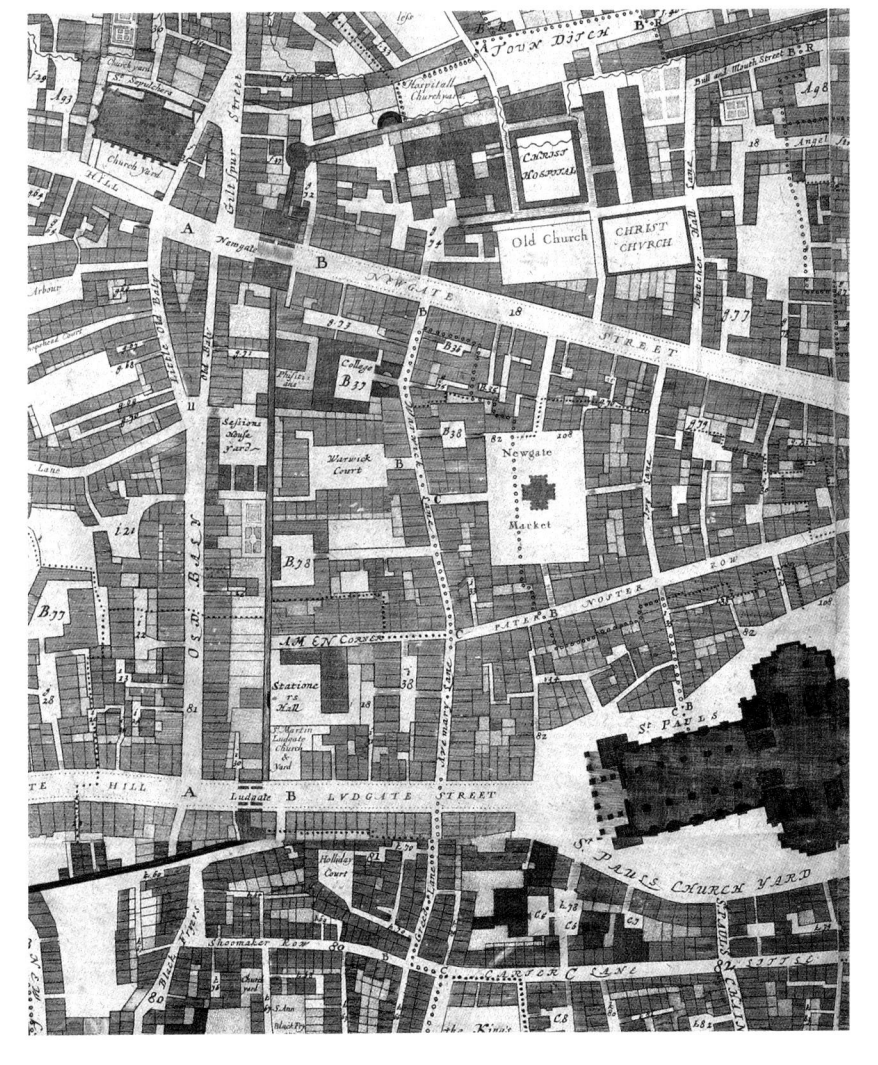

Detail of the Ogilby and Morgan map of London, 1676, showing the Old Bailey. The Blacksmiths' Company's property was close to St Sepulchre's church and St Bartholomew's hospital, beyond Newgate.

© THE BRITISH LIBRARY BOARD, MAPS, CRACE II, 61

Staff-head presented by Past Prime Warden Charles Ravenhill in 1879. It is still used by the Beadle.

given consent for a plaque to be affixed to the wall of their headquarters' building in Lambeth Hill, to read: 'On this site stood the Blacksmiths' Hall, 1494–1785'. This was damaged by the Blitz in 1941; the present plaque, which reads 'site of the Blacksmiths' Hall 1668–1785', ignores the medieval predecessor.

At the meeting of the Court on 4 January 1821 the Company replied to a letter from the Secretary of the Commissioners appointed by Parliament for investigating charities by saying that the only properties charged with any charitable donation that they possessed were the George public house, known formerly as the Crown and Hoop, without Newgate, and nearby tenements in the Old Bailey and Fleet Lane. On 6 November 1823 it was agreed that when the lease expired next Midsummer the George should be pulled down and rebuilt and the tenant offered a new lease of 61 years, while the other four houses should be let for 31 years. At the same time, the Company considered selling their houses on St Andrew's Hill (which they had purchased for the rental income rather than for the purpose of charitable donations) to the Municipal Commissioners in order to widen the street and other local improvements. On 1 January 1835 the Company were offered £1,060 for this, a bid that was raised later to £1,147 7s. 0d., but on 5 March 1835 the Company asked for £1,600, and no agreement was reached. Two years later, the houses on St Andrew's Hill were advertised for sale, but the Company eventually settled for a new lease.

On 5 January 1854 a Committee of Investigation into the affairs of the Company reported that the 'freehold house called the George Inn, Old Bailey' had been leased at Midsummer 1824 at the rent of £100 for 61 years. Three freehold houses in Fleet Lane (built in the year 1828 upon the site where four houses formerly stood) had been let for 61 years in 1828 for £36, three freehold houses numbered 32, 34 and 35 Saint Andrew's at Hill, formerly known as Puddle Wharf and Puddle Dock, had been leased for 31 years in 1837 for £53, while number 33 had been leased for 21 years in 1852 for £25. The committee reported further that the freehold house at number 4 New High Road, leading from Hammersmith Bridge Road to Barnes, which had been leased in 1847 for 99 years at £13, had been purchased by the Company on 18 February 1853, and that a freehold lease of 24 Cursitor Street, off Chancery Lane, had been taken in 1852 for 21 years £60. In 1846 a freehold house at 19 King Street, Finsbury, had been leased for £50 for 7¼ years. Finally, they also noted that the Company had invested £521 4s. 3d. in Consolidated Stocks and £64 in the Irish Society. A legacy of £20 brought the Company's annual income to £386 1s. 11d.; in the previous year expenditure had totalled £353 3s. 2d.

Further information about the Company's properties is provided by the Court minute books towards the end of the nineteenth century. On 4 January 1883 Mr George Hayton, the lessee of a warehouse at 32/33 Saint Andrew's Hill, was allowed to conduct his business as a wholesale wine and spirit merchant there provided he increased the fire insurance cover. On 7 December 1893 the Company's properties in the Old Bailey and Fleet Lane were greatly damaged by fire, but the insurance that was paid enabled structural and other alterations to be made and a new lease agreed the following year for The George, Old Bailey, and 29–31 Fleet Lane. By this time, the Company also owned property in Christopher Street, Finsbury, identified in later minute books as number 13. Finally, and more surprisingly, on 1 June 1899 it was reported that the freehold ground rent on Hove Lodge Mansion, Hove Street, Hove, Brighton, had been purchased by the Company for £3,325. It was estimated that leasing this property would pay the Company 'a little over £3 12s. 0d. per cent', and £2,886 12s. 0d. Consolidated Stocks had been sold to help pay for it.

Proposals for Reform

The Corporation of London and the livery companies remained largely untouched by reform schemes urged by outsiders. The City of London was exempted from the provisions of the Municipal Reform Act (1835) and it was as late as 1856 that membership of a livery company ceased to confer economic privileges within the City. After 1832 liverymen no longer had the exclusive right to elect the City's four members of Parliament, but they retained a vote until 1918. In 1848 a printed poster named 82 liverymen of the Blacksmiths' Company who were 'entitled to vote in the election of Members for the City of London'. All but one liveryman who lived at Layton, Essex, resided within Greater London, but of these only seventeen were from within the City walls. The majority came from north or east London, but 21 lived south of the river

Thames in such places as Greenwich, Deptford or Bermondsey. The Company were still clearly 'of London' at this time.

In fighting off a challenge from a parliamentary bill on electoral reform in 1852, the Lord Mayor sent a questionnaire requesting details of membership from each company. The Blacksmiths replied that 76 of their liverymen were entitled to vote at elections, while eight liverymen and 74 freemen had no such entitlement. During the previous seven years only three men had been admitted to the livery and only 18 freemen had been admitted to the company.

On 9 February 1860 a Special Meeting of the Blacksmiths' Court defiantly expressed the opinion that:

> the Bill now in Parliament purporting to be for the better regulation of the City of London, altho' professing to abolish such Customs and Privileges as injuriously affect Trade, ignore the whole body of Livery composed of Ten thousand of the most influential Merchants Bankers and Traders of the first City in the World, depriving them of their Municipal Franchise. That it destroys all Royal Charters, Grants and Letters Patent now in force relating to the Corporation of the City of London which is manifestly unjust. And this Meeting strongly protests against such a measure and pledges itself to use every lawful means to prevent it passing into Law.

The Company agreed to present a petition to the House of Commons.

During the 1870s various reformers associated with the Liberal Party attacked the Corporation of London and the livery companies by seeking to annul their ancient royal charters and to appropriate company funds for utilitarian purposes. Led by William James, a radical MP, they moved for an enquiry into the resources of the 89 livery companies and to ascertain how much was devoted to technical education. The livery companies realised that if they were to survive, they would have to recognise the 'altered circumstances and necessities' of the modern world. Many companies now sought to renew contact with their former trades. They had lost their previous authority, but they could justify their existence by supporting technical education for young craftsmen and by offering prizes and medals for outstanding achievements.

In 1880 the radical reformers succeeded in persuading Gladstone's Liberal Government to establish a Royal Commission on the Livery Companies of the City of London. Perhaps this was a classic example of how to shelve a problem, for the commissioners who were appointed were never going to reach unanimous agreement, but it certainly helped to persuade liverymen of the need to do something to partly satisfy their critics. The commissioners began by issuing a questionnaire, but it was not until 1882 that they commenced their oral hearings. The twelve great companies each made detailed returns and 59 of the minor companies made shorter ones.

At the meeting of the Court on 21 October 1882 the Clerk was asked to prepare the Blacksmiths' return. He noted that the Company had 81 liverymen and 83 freemen and an annual income of £684. Altogether, the London livery companies had 7,319 liverymen and funds amounting to between £750,000 and £800,000, of which about £200,000 was held in trust for charities. Like many other small companies, the Blacksmiths had no income to dispense in this way.

The Commissioners were also informed, in answer to their questions, that the freedom of the Blacksmiths' Company was obtainable by servitude (as an apprentice who had completed his term), by patrimony (following a father into the trade), or by redemption (through the sponsorship of a liveryman of at least four years standing and the payment of a fee). Formerly, a quarterage of four shillings per annum was demanded, but this caused much trouble in the collection. Women had once been admitted to the Company, but none had joined during the last twenty years. For 30 years previous to 1833 the admissions or calls to the livery had often been just one or two a year, the highest numbers being in the years 1805, 1810 and 1818, when 10, 11 and 10 members respectively were admitted. During the same period new freemen numbered from six to 21 a year. In 1834 about three-fifths of the Livery were, or had been, smiths, and nearly one-half of the whole Company were of the trade. By 1883, however, in answer to the Commission's question as to how many members of the trade were members of the Blacksmiths' Company, the Clerk replied 'Nine'. Such was the decline of the Company's old responsibilities that only three apprentices had been admitted in the past ten years. Nor did the Company do anything 'to subsidise or encourage education, whether general or technical'. By the 1880s the Blacksmiths' Company had reached the lowest point in its long history.

The return made to the Commissioners also stated that 'The Company is not possessed of plate, pictures or furniture, but a loving cup, in private hands, of silver', donated in 1665 by Christopher Pym. The Blacksmiths were not a rich corporation and the only city charity it possessed was that founded in June 1557 by Edward Prestyn, who left five houses in Fleet Lane and Old Bailey,

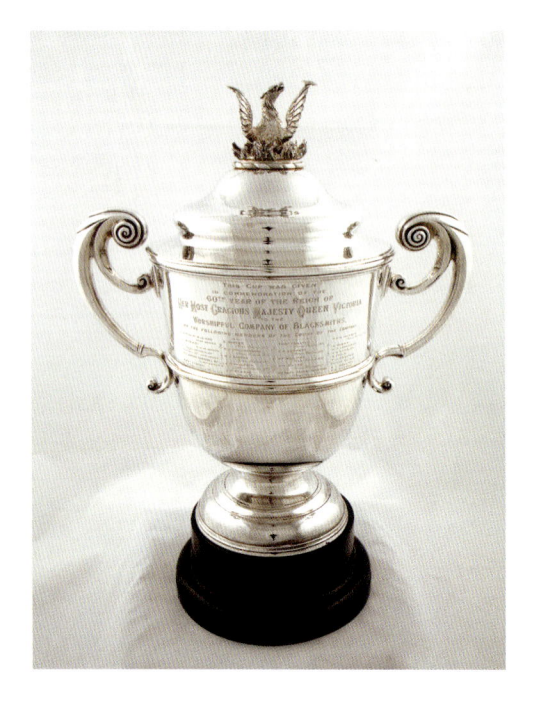

Cup presented by 24 members of the Court of the Company to commemorate the Diamond Jubilee of Queen Victoria in 1897. The front is engraved with the Company's Coat of Arms and Motto. The finial on the cover shows the phoenix arising from the flames. It was made in London.

charged with the bestowal of four shillings per annum among the 'poor artists' of the Company. The Blacksmiths received a rental from these premises of £136 a year, yet paid in charity £12 per annum each to 12 poor persons. The Company privately purchased some other small properties, the rents of which helped with such donations. In 1881 the Company had just seven pensioners, including four widows.

When their deliberations were finished, the Royal Commission was unable to issue an agreed report, so a majority report (critical of the livery companies) and a minority report (vindicating the companies' stewardship of their charitable funds and their role in helping to contribute to education, social science and human progress) were published in 1884. They had little immediate effect on the London livery companies, but did help to raise awareness of the need to do more for the modern successors of their ancient trades.

New Initiatives

While the Royal Commission was making its enquiries, the Company began to contribute to charities that it had not previously supported. On 29 July 1882 it was agreed that five guineas per annum should be paid to the funds of the Iron, Hardware, and Metal Trades Pension Society, and small gifts were made to a variety of other charities which had no connection with the trade, including two guineas to the funds of the Thames Angling Preservation Society. Meanwhile, annual grants continued to be made to the Royal Metal Trades Pension Society.

On 4 January 1883 the Court minutes recorded:

> That we are of the opinion that much good might accrue by steps being taken to bring before the working members of the Trade and the Trade Apprentices the fact that the Company is very desirous of assisting such an exhibition of Blacksmiths' work as shall redound to the credit of the Trade and of the Company.

The Prime Warden's Badge. On 7 July 1870 the Company accepted a badge for the Prime Warden which had been donated by James Abbis, JP. The 'very handsome badge' was made of 18 carat yellow gold and enamel, and it weighs over 100 grams. It depicts the Arms and Crest of the Company, mounted in Victorian Gothic style, adorned by 'A Phoenix in Glory' and the Company's motto. The badge hangs from an 18 carat gold chain which was presented to the Company by Past Prime Warden Charles Ravenhill in the same year.

It was eventually agreed that the first prize for a journeyman was to be £10 and the freedom of the Company; the second and third prizes were £7 10s. 0d. and £5, respectively. Two money prizes, bronze medals and certificates of merit were offered for youths employed in a smith's work shop in each of three sections: under the age of 17; 17–19; and 19–21. Entry to the competition was open to anyone within the United Kingdom. The Exhibition was held in the Ironmongers' Hall in 1889 and was judged by Ewing Matheson, Esquire, a Member of the Institute of Civil Engineers and was judged a great success. An outside opinion was that, 'Like most of the first exhibitions that have been held for the promotion of technical education, the Blacksmiths' has not been an extensive one', but the 28 exhibitors had produced work of good quality'. The total cost of the exhibition came to £146 1s. 11d.

Another initiative was to honour leading members of the Institutes of Civil Engineers and Mechanical Engineers. On 22 May 1890 a Special Court held at the Guildhall conferred Honorary Freedoms and the Livery to Sir John Fowler, Sir Benjamin Baker, and Sir William Arrol in commemoration of the successful completion of the Forth Bridge. They were presented with iron caskets inscribed with the Company's arms and an inscription.

The Company had insufficient wealth to do much more. In 1889 the county councils that had been created the year before were empowered to levy a penny rate for technical education and to provide scholarships. When the London County Council wrote to the livery companies for support, the Blacksmiths replied on 6 October 1892 that 'from want of funds the Company have no institution under their control in which Technical or Manual Instruction is given, but hold periodically an Exhibition of Hammered Iron Ware when the Freedom of the Company and money prizes are given to successful Exhibitors'. On 6 May 1893, in reply to another letter from the Clerk of the London County Council regarding 'Technical Education in London', asking whether the Company was willing to make a contribution towards the necessary expenses of the Technical Education Board, the Company replied that 'the funds at our disposal are being applied to technical education purposes'. Later, they felt unable to help with the promotion of Fulham Polytechnic. Likewise, in 1893 when the Carpenters' Company asked for their co-operation in the running of their newly opened Trades' Training Schools in Great Titchfield Street, where instruction was given in a wide variety of building crafts, they felt unable to help, and 'because of the state of the funds' they turned down one of their own member's suggestion that they offer £30. Several other livery companies contributed to the scheme.

On 2 March 1893 a committee was formed to arrange a new Exhibition of Hammered Iron Ware in the Ironmongers' Hall 'to promote technical education among the rising generation of the trade, art or mystery'. This was again to take the form of a Prize Competition for Journeymen, Apprentices or Youths working in Smiths' Shops in the United Kingdom. By 31 January 1894 over 250 applications for particulars of prizes had been received. The Lord Mayor opened the exhibition on 11 April 1894 and said 'that all the City Companies would do well to emulate' the Blacksmiths' Company's enterprise. These exhibitions were the beginnings of the Company's involvement in sponsoring the blacksmith's craft at shows and exhibitions. On 7 March 1895, for instance, they agreed to nominate a judge in the Handicraft Competitions held by The International Building Trades Exhibition Company.

Company business

Meanwhile, the Company's social life centred on the 'Ladies dinner', such as that held at the Star and Garter, Richmond, in 1879. Three years later, it was agreed that 'the Summer Entertainment to the members of the Court and their Ladies, and to the Livery paying their quarterage, and their Ladies', should be on board the Thames pleasure boat, the *Maria Wood*, in July. In 1889 and 1890 the *Maria Wood* was engaged again, for trips from Kingston to Sunbury and back, with gifts of 'perfume for the Ladies, as usual'. In the following two years, the summer entertainment was held at Windsor and the Crystal Palace. Then, in 1895 the Whitehall Rooms at the Hotel Metropole were chosen, with 'vocalists' and The Delina's Orchestral Band engaged to play a selection of music during the dinner and the concert afterwards.

Working blacksmiths still sometimes played a prominent role in the affairs of the Company, but no information is available that reveals the occupations of other members of the Court, other than one or two colonels. Court meetings were now held at the Guildhall and the Company's records were stored there in the vaults. An occasional apprentice was formally bound, and the Company's pensioners were paid their quarter's money and five shillings each from the poor box. In 1892–93 the Company received £1,598 14*s*. 6*d*. and spent £1,196 10*s*. 11*d*., but in 1898 it was stated that fees payable on admission were now considerably less than formerly, the average over the last three years being £77. Invitations to the January dinner in 1896 were sent to the Masters of the Ironmongers', Vintners', Armourers & Braziers', Cutlers', Clockmakers', and Farriers' Companies. Then, in 1897 the Company sent a Loyal Address to Her Majesty and gratefully accepted the offer of Mr Arthur William Elwood of 9 Kennington Park Gardens to 'make and present to the Company a specimen of Hammered Iron Work in commemoration of the Queen's Diamond Jubilee'. Arthur Elwood was to become a prominent Liveryman in the Company during the first half of the twentieth century.

The Court minutes record regular attention to the Company's properties on St Andrew's Hill, the Old Bailey, 13 Christopher Street, 24 Cursitor Street, Barnes Villas at 4 Lonsdale Road, and Hove Lodge Mansions, whose combined gross rentals in 1914 amounted to £525. But three centuries after the Company had been forced to invest in King James I's Ulster Plantations, their involvement there came to an end. The Irish Land Act (1903) prompted so many applications for redemption that the Vintners Company (the head of the group that included the Blacksmiths) decided that the time had come to sell. In 1910–11 the Blacksmiths' Company received £77 15s. 5d. from the redemption of rent charges, which it proceeded to invest in Consolidated Stock. The connection with the Vintners' Company came to an end, and in 1909 invitations to the Court Dinner were restricted to the Masters of the Ironmongers, Armourers & Braziers, Cutlers, Painter-Stainers, Farriers, Clockmakers, and the Tylers & Brickmakers.

On 6 January 1910 the report of the committee on the present state and prospects of the Company's finances stated that the annual income was £1,268, exclusive of the fees payable on admission, which averaged £112 per annum. The annual expenditure to which the Company was liable came to £1,341, but the average expenditure over the last three years had amounted to £1,406. The

Silver Cup. This two handled cup and cover on a square plinth, engraved with the Company's Arms, was made in London in 1905 by D. & J. Welby and presented to the Company by Walter Cranmer Hetherington, a member of the Court of Assistants, in 1955.

Loving Cup designed by J.E. Stapley of London in 1957, and engraved with the Company's Coat of Arms. It was purchased by the Company out of a legacy from Past Prime Warden Edwin Albert Curtis.

Charger. A silver gilt electro formed piece of 1871 by Frederick Elkington of Birmingham, which was presented to the Company by Prime Warden Walter Cranmer Hetherington in 1963. The centre is decorated with mythological masks and figures, the border in the Egyptian revival style.

Rosebowl presented by several members of the Livery on the occasion of Queen Victoria's Diamond Jubilee. It was made in London by Alstons and Hellam of Cornhill.

committee's recommendation that the April dinner for the Court and Livery should be abolished until further notice was agreed. The October Livery dinner at Ironmongers' Hall continued to be held, however. All dinners were suspended during the years of the First World War.

The Company did not thrive during the late Victorian and Edwardian period, but its members were determined to hang on to their privileges if they could. On 6 December 1917 the Prime Warden reported that he had attended a meeting of the Committee of the Livery Companies for securing the retention of the Livery vote under the Representation of the People Bill, which proposed to extend the national franchise to all men and to women over the age of 30. The Company agreed to contribute 20 guineas towards the committee's expenses, but the livery companies were fighting a lost cause.

Wider Contacts

In the opening years of the twentieth century the Blacksmiths' Company continued to award a silver medal and £1 worth of books to the Smiths' Class at the Great Titchfield Street Trades Training School for the best specimen of hammered iron work. But this was the only scheme that they sponsored before the First World War. In 1907 17 petitions for grants from various smiths were placed on the table, and in the following year another 22 were treated in the same way.

In 1922 a London County Council Enquiry 'as to the work of an Educational nature carried out by the City Livery Companies since 1880' produced a brief response from the Blacksmiths' Company. They began by saying that 20 guineas had been given to the City & Guilds of London Institute for the Advancement of Technical Education some 20 years ago. This institution was formed in 1880, about the time that the Royal Commission began its enquiries, when some of the City's livery companies began to assist local technical colleges in various parts of the country. In 1883 their Central Technical College was opened at South Kensington on an 87-acre site that had been bought by the 1851 Great Exhibition Commissioners for 'purposes of art and science'. The earliest three-year full-time courses started in February 1885.

The Company also noted in its responses that it had held two exhibitions of hammered iron work in the City since 1890 when awards consisting of the Freedom of the Company, Silver and Bronze Medals, and money had been made; for many years the Company had given a money prize with a Bronze Medal in connection with the Smiths' Class held at the Great Titchfield Trades' Training Schools; students of the Iron and Steel Institute were offered annually the Freedom and a Gold Medal for some original work connected with the metallurgy of iron and steel; and the Company had arranged with the Iron and Steel Institute for lectures to be given from time to time. William Henry Ellis, Past President of the Institute, gave the first in 1921.

The Iron and Steel Institute had been founded in 1869 for the discussion of practical and scientific subjects bearing upon the manufacture and use of iron and steel. The papers presented at its periodical meetings were published in the Institute's *Proceedings*. On 30 March 1871 it reported that:

> Notwithstanding the pre-eminent scale on which the mineral and metallic industries of Great Britain are conducted in practice, it must nevertheless be admitted that, as a rule, we have hitherto been long and far behind our continental neighbours in respect to possessing institutions calculated to aid in developing or advancing the scientific or practical bearings of such subjects, or to afford the means of intercommunication between those occupied or interested in such

pursuits. To this rule, however, we now have, at least, one honourable exception in the case of the Iron and Steel Institute, now holding its second annual meeting in London, and the establishment of which, in 1869, must be looked upon by all interested in the application of science to the arts, not only as a decided step forward in the right direction, but may even be regarded as inaugurating a new era in the history of the so important iron and steel manufactures of Great Britain.

A report on 28 March 1872 noted that:

The Third Annual Meeting of the Iron and Steel Institute was last week held in London, under the presidency of Mr. Henry Bessemer, and has been numerously attended by representatives, not only of the principal iron and steel works in the United Kingdom, but also by those of many of the most important metallurgical establishments on the Continent, which in several instances have sent special delegates to this meeting. It will perhaps be remembered that the Iron and Steel Institute was founded barely three years ago, and that upon the occasion of the Inaugural Address, delivered by the first president (the Duke of Devonshire), it had then only received the adherence of some two hundred gentlemen connected with the trade; whereas, on this occasion, notwithstanding that the rules of the society only allow the admission of those either practically engaged in the manufacture or application of iron and steel, or connected therewith by their scientific attainments, it has increased so rapidly in this short interval as to number at present about five hundred members, including in this list nearly all the influence and talent associated with the iron and steel industries of Great Britain.

It was not until after the First World War, however, that the Blacksmiths' Company became involved with the Institute. This link was an initiative of Sir Walter Henry Harris, the Prime Warden for two years, from 1918 to 1920. Harris was a new broom who had influential contacts. In 1918 he met Sir William Beardmore, Bart, the President of the Iron and Steel Institute, who expressed his willingness to assist the Company in any scheme to further the craft. On 7 May 1919 the Blacksmiths' Company presented the Honorary Freedom and Livery of the Company to M. Eugene Schneider, head of the

The river Thames at London was a significant centre of ship-building and repair. This photograph shows a blacksmith's forge worked by the Blackwall Engineering Company in Poplar for ship repair work until the firm closed in 1987.
MUSEUM OF LONDON

Creusot Works in France, the current President of the Iron and Steel Institute, and to Sir William Beardmore. The ceremony took place in the Guildhall and was followed by lunch at the Innholders' Hall. Sir Walter Harris thanked the Council of the Iron and Steel Institute for attending in large numbers and went on to say that, 'When we first approached the Iron and Steel Institute, it was with a view – if I may put it frankly – to endeavour to bring about a state of affairs which meant that livery companies of the City wished to justify their existence'. Because of modern improvements, 'the manual blacksmith seems … to have gone back to the business of shoeing, but even that man has been supplied with machine-made shoes'. But now:

> The Iron and Steel Institute have done us the honour, and allow us to present annually a gold medal and the Freedom of the Company to an individual who is deemed most worthy of the distinction which is in our power to confer. At the same time … we shall be bringing

into our ranks an operative … In the course of time we shall have a much stronger body of persons associated with the trade who will be members of the Company than we have in the past. We have many good men on the Court of Assistants, but, like myself, they are not all blacksmiths.

On 5 October 1922 Sir William Henry Ellis of the Atlas Works, Sheffield, President of the Iron and Steel Institute in 1923 and former Master of the Cutlers' Company of Hallamshire, was awarded the Freedom of the Company together with the Gold Medal. In his acceptance speech he said that he was anxious that the Blacksmiths' Company should again become the real guardian of its craft. On the same occasion, Mr Francis Samuelson of Brackenbrough Hall, Thirsk, the President of the Iron and Steel Institute, was admitted as a Member of the Company. On 28 March 1924 the Secretary of the Iron and Steel Institute submitted two names, as requested, of men who were admitted to the freedom and livery. This worked well at first, but in the years of the Great Depression new men were reluctant to come forward. On 7 May 1931 the Iron and Steel Institute 'felt able to nominate one member only this year for Admission to the Company – Mr John Spilman Walton, Port Talbot, Glamorganshire'. In the following year no nomination was received.

In 1920, the new Prime Warden, Colonel A. Tubby induced Sir Robert A. Hadfield, Bart, FRS, DSc, 'one of the leading men in the steel industry', to join the Livery. On 7 July 1927 members of the Court received an invitation from Hadfield to visit his East Hecla steelworks and other iron and steel works at Sheffield. Hadfield was a brilliant metallurgist and entrepreneur, a former Master Cutler of the Hallamshire Company, and the President of the Iron and Steel Institute when they had visited Sheffield in 1905. Eight members took up his offer and Hadfield insisted on paying their train fares and on singing the Blacksmiths' Song to them at the luncheon that he provided; he also asked for permission to look through the Company's old books at the Guildhall. Hadfield was a Liberal and an enlightened employer who was keenly interested in furthering technical education. He worked a 16-hour day and was once described in the engineering press as the 'hardest working man under the sun'. On 3 October 1929, when the Blacksmiths' Company elected him an Honorary Member of the Court of Assistants, he wrote from his London home, 22 Carlton House Terrace, to say that he esteemed the honour, but that he was too busy to attend many meetings. On 20 March 1929 a second lecture was given at the Carpenters' Hall by Sir William Henry Ellis (who had helped with the Sheffield visit). The Company's links with Sheffield were strengthened further during the following year when the Prime Warden was invited to the Cutlers' Feast, where he received 'generous hospitality' from the Master Cutler (Mr Peter Brown), Sir Robert Hadfield, Sir William Ellis and other friends. When Ellis died in 1945, he left the Blacksmiths' Company a bequest of £2,500.

Despite their amicable relationship with the Cutlers' Company of Hallamshire, the Blacksmiths had no links with The Incorporated Company of Smiths of Newcastle-upon-Tyne, an ancient fraternity, whose earliest ordinance dates from 1436. This company represented the three branches of the trade in Newcastle, namely: blacksmiths and farriers; anchor smiths; and locksmiths or white smiths. Their hall adjoined the Blackfriars in Newcastle, where they met yearly on St Loy's day. Intriguingly, they had the same arms, crest and motto as the Blacksmiths' Company. In 1827 the company consisted of 78 members, and their annual income was only about £40.

County Shows and the Rural Industries Bureau

The Company's first involvement in a show organised by a county agricultural society was with the Hertfordshire Rural Industries Exhibition in 1927 at Hatfield, when they donated a prize of a bronze medal and two guineas for the best work by a smith. The success of this venture led to long-term co-operation with the Hertfordshire Institute of Agriculture. Mr Arthur Elwood, a working blacksmith who had been Prime Warden in 1924, held a course of lectures for smiths in St Albans and acted as the judge for the exhibition. In 1931 he reported that he was greatly pleased with the 21 exhibits, which exceeded the quantity and quality of previous years.

On 4 October 1928 Colonel Tubby, a Past Prime Warden, commented on articles in the press, especially one in *The Times* of 20 September on 'Fostering the Craft of the Village Blacksmith', and asked if they could join in 'this modern movement' in conjunction with the Rural Industries Co-operative Society. The Rural Industries Bureau, which had been established in 1921 by the Ministry of Agriculture, aimed to develop rural industries by providing technical advice and assistance to country workshops. It also published various booklets and reports and the quarterly magazine, *Rural Industries*. Its first technical officer was Arthur Elwood.

In 1929 the Company offered prizes for hammered ironwork at the British

Industries Fair organized by the British Institute of Industrial Art at the White City, but not enough entries were attracted, so instead it was agreed that a grant of £20 per annum should be made to assist in the payment of the fees of not less than 20 village blacksmiths for attendance at lectures organized by county councils. The Rural Industries Bureau expressed their appreciation but said that as fees were not charged for such lectures the money might be well spent in other ways. Nottinghamshire asked if the grant could be used instead for the purchase of a forge for smiths' classes at the Newark School of Science and Art; Kent asked if it could be used to defray organisation expenses in connection with pioneer lectures; and Hertfordshire asked if it could go towards the expenses of smiths who had to travel long distances. Eventually, the Company agreed that the annual £20 grant could be used at the discretion of the Bureau.

The following year, the Rural Industries Bureau suggested that £5 should be awarded to Monmouthshire Rural Community Council to pay the travelling expenses of a tutor (a local smith) and the hire of a room for a course of demonstrations of acetylene welding and a short course in book-keeping; that £4 should be given to Hampshire RCC for the travelling expenses of blacksmiths attending from a distance courses in acetylene welding and cutting, which had been arranged in seven villages; and that £3 should be awarded to Derbyshire RCC for the fees and expenses of an examiner in farriery, after a series of classes arranged by the Community Council and the Local Education Authority, who had paid the fees of the lecturer and part of the travelling expenses of the eight smiths. Later, £3 was given to Nottinghamshire RCC for the travelling expenses of two smiths to a class in wrought ironwork at the County Technical College, Newark-on-Trent, and £5 was granted towards a course of instruction organized by a smith in Truro, Cornwall. In the following year, awards were made to help the Bath and West Show at Bristol, the Royal Counties Agricultural Show at Portsmouth, the Three Counties Show, at Hereford, and the Lincolnshire Show at Lincoln. In 1932 letter the Rural Industries Bureau reported that small grants had been made: £2 to Mr Mayo of Newnham (Gloucestershire), for the purchase of a Punching Machine; £3 to Gainsborough Council of Social Service for the purchase of a Pillar Drilling Machine to be used by smiths working under their auspice; and £1 10s. 0d. to Mr Cousins of Stamford for the purchase of a vice and metal tools. In these small ways, the Company provided welcome assistance to rural blacksmiths in different parts of the kingdom.

The Company was beginning to take an interest in a number of county

Decorated salver made in London and presented in 1858 to George Scammell, the Chairman of the Coal, Corn and Finance Committee of the City of London. In 1939 it was given to the Company in his memory by his grandson and namesake.

agricultural shows. In 1934 it awarded diplomas for exhibits at the Bath and West and Southern Counties Show at Oxford; the Royal Agricultural Society's Show at Ipswich; the Royal Welsh Agricultural Show at Llandudno; the Rutland Agricultural Show at Oakham; and the Bakewell Agricultural Show in Derbyshire. Most of these shows already had a long history; indeed, the Royal Agricultural Society of England had been founded in 1838 and had long pursued a policy of holding its annual show on a peripatetic basis in order to bring the latest ideas to general public attention.

Another proposal that was considered by the Company was a scheme for the national registration of smiths. On 6 October 1932 this was put to the Iron and Steel Institute, who expressed guarded interest in 'a movement intended to encourage the work of the smith in rural districts now that the ordinary blacksmith is fast disappearing from the villages'. They pointed out, however, that all the large manufacturing centres had evening classes in schools to improve trade qualifications and for obtaining certificates of proficiency,

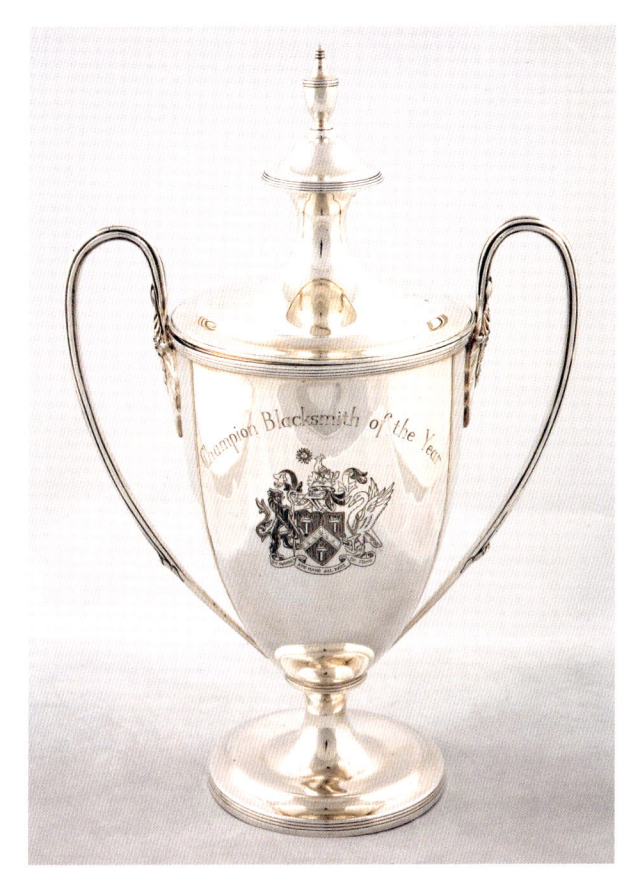

The Captain Beale Cup was made in London and was presented to the Company in 1935, as the award for the '*Champion Blacksmith of the Year*', by Captain Alan Beale, MBE, MC, Croix de Guerre (Belges), a farmer in Kent who supported the Kent Show and became Prime Warden in 1953. His father, Louis Steven Beale was Prime Warden in 1933, and his son, Alan John Beale became Prime Warden in 1974, and later the Father of the Company.

and that if the Company held independent examinations and tests this might overlap with the technical education provided by the Board of Education. The Institute's advice, therefore, was to link up with and encourage existing schemes for training craftsmen rather than to try to organise new ones. The Company took the hint and abandoned the scheme as impractical. On 5 January 1933 they noted that 'ample opportunity was available to obtain instruction and help through existing Guilds and Institutions in the various centres of manufacture and that diplomas and rewards are granted by such. The Company is not in a position either in personnel or finance to institute and pursue an independent course of instruction and examination'. They decided that their efforts were best channelled, as before, through the Rural Industries Bureau and Mr Arthur Elwood's good work and connections in Hertfordshire, together with support for other events that featured the work of blacksmiths. In 1936, for example, the Company donated a prize of two guineas at the Olympia Building Exhibition.

Properties and business

The First World War had interrupted the social life of the Company, and as late as 4 January 1923 it was judged that 'the time for a Livery Dinner had not yet arrived'. In the following year, however, such a dinner was held at the Innholders' Hall, where accommodation was limited to 70, so only two seats each could be booked. On 1 October 1931 the Company agreed to appoint an Honorary Chaplain to say Grace at banquets and, if possible, to attend the Courts when Affirmations were required to be made. The Revd Herbert Stephenson Payne, MA, Precentor of Worcester Cathedral, Citizen and Blacksmith, was duly elected to the post.

In 1929 the property at 24 Cursitor Street, off Chancery Lane, was sold. Then, on 2 June 1932 the Company took the important decision to sell The George, Old Bailey, and numbers 29, 30 and 31 Fleet Lane for £20,000 and to invest the proceeds in Two-and-a-half Per Cent Consolidated Stock. No reason for selling their oldest property was given in the minutes. On 5 January 1933 the Company's stock that was registered at the Bank of England was valued at £36,252 7s. 11d. When the Company's London properties were inspected in 1936, they consisted only of 13 Christopher Street, Finsbury, 31–34 St Andrew's Hill, and Hove Lodge Mansions at Brighton.

In June 1933 the Company were approached by the Revd P. B. 'Tubby' Clayton, the Vicar of All Hallows-by-the-Tower, the clergyman who had founded Toc-H during the First World War, who asked for permission to copy the Company's Arms on a small panel decorating the new undercoft in his church. Two years later, this led to the Company commissioning Arthur Elwood to design wrought iron gates before the altar in the undercroft, bearing the Company's Arms, and John Bryan, a craftsman in Hertfordshire who had recently gained the Company's silver medal, to make them. The Court minutes noted that 'there can be no question that the gates will attract attention to the Company and serve to demonstrate the useful work that we are now doing to revive what is one of the oldest and most deeply rooted of English handicrafts'. The total cost to the Company was £112, but the Livery subscribed £143. The church was almost destroyed by bombing in the Second World War, but in 1966 the Blacksmiths' Company paid for the present gates, made by Messrs George Lister & Sons Ltd, with enamelling by Messrs France Signs.

On the outbreak of the Second World War the Company's minute book was deposited with the Midland Bank, 20 Eastcheap, and entries were not resumed until 4 October 1945. In the immediate post-war years the Company functioned much as before. The Iron and Steel Institute continued to nominate honorary members, the Company's properties were repaired and maintained, an annual grant of ten guineas was made to the City and Guilds of London Institute, relations with the Rural Industries Bureau were re-established, and in the 1950s medals and diplomas for outstanding work were presented again and prizes were competed for at royal and county agricultural shows. From 1954 a challenge shield for 'the best exhibition of the blacksmith's art' was offered at the Kent County Agricultural Show. On 7 July 1955 the Company agreed to pay nine annual charitable gifts of five guineas each and seven at two guineas each. The Company's social activities were also revived, though an attempt to organize a ball to commemorate the coronation of Queen Elizabeth II in 1953 floundered because the planning was left so late that no City Hall was still available during Coronation Year. Three years later, the Prime Warden was concerned 'at the laxity that members of the Livery and their guests had shown in wearing Dinner Jackets at the Livery Banquet'; full evening dress was insisted upon. Various company halls, including the Grocers' and the Fishmongers', were hired for the annual banquet, until 1967, when the Mansion House was first used; since then the event has usually been held there.

Significant changes in the Company's investments were made in the post-war years. In 1946 the long lease on Barnes Villas, 4 Lonsdale Road, ran out and was not renewed. On 17 January 1956 a recommendation of the Finance Committee that the Company's holding of £38,344 16s. 11d. in 2.5 Consolidated Stock and £850 in 3.5 per cent Conversion Stock should be sold and reinvested in Government Stocks and/or first class Industrial Securities was agreed. More significantly, on 29 January 1957 the Clerk reported the completion of the sale of the Hove Lodge Mansions for £5,002 16s. 10d., a sum that was deposited with the Midland Bank, Eastcheap. Finally, on 6 June 1967 the property at 13 Christopher Street was sold for £15,000. The only property that the Company still owned was that on St Andrew's Hill.

5 The Modern Company of Blacksmiths

The Livery

The Worshipful Company of Blacksmiths continues to support its ancient craft, participates in the civic life of the City of London, makes charitable donations, and provides convivial dinners and social events for the Livery. It remains one of the smaller London livery companies and ranks 40th in order of precedence, but it is better placed than most in actively preserving its links with craftsmen who work in the tradition of those who formed the Company over 700 years ago. Its major regret is that it does not possess its own hall.

On 3 October 1968 Dr G. E. K. Blythe addressed the Court on the subject of 'securing finances for the re-building of a Blacksmiths' Livery Company Hall'. His sentiments were warmly received by members of the Court and a Planning Committee for a New Hall was formed, but no progress was made at that time. Four years later, the Company investigated the possibility of converting one of the City churches which were being made redundant, but again the idea came to nought.

A serious attempt to provide a new hall was instigated in 1988 on the site of the Company's only remaining property, a freehold plot of land on St Andrew's Hill, close to Blackfriars station and the Church of St Andrew-by-the-Wardrobe. On 26 May 1988 the Company submitted a planning application for Conservation Area Consent to demolish a public house and a warehouse tenanted by a paper company in order to erect a six-storey building designed by Green Lloyd Architects which would provide a Livery Hall, public house, and offices. The original design was an interpretation of the (demolished) Baynard's Castle, which once stood close by, but this was not long after Prince Charles had publicly criticised a proposed design for development near St

Father's badge. This 18 carat yellow gold and black enamel badge with three white gold applied crown and hammer motifs is worn by the Father of the Company. It was presented by Hubert Shepherd MBE, the Father in 1966.

The 'Indian Necklace', which is worn by the Prime Warden's lady. The origin and provenance of the necklace is unknown, but it is believed to be more likely Middle Eastern, possibly Persian. It was presented to the Company by Major F. H. Humphris RAMC LRCPL, Prime Warden 1941–43. It is turquoise on the reverse.

Paul's, so the City planners were cautious. The Company was directed instead to design a building that would replace exactly the existing facade, but this meant loss of lettable office space. The new application was approved, but at this stage Bass Charrington regretfully concluded that the development of their portion was not appropriate at the time, so the Company had to think again. The early 1990s' recession stopped many developments in the City, and the Company was obliged to suspend its plans, hoping that it could implement them when market conditions improved. The impetus was lost, and it was decided, reluctantly, that the proposed accommodation would have been large enough for Court meetings but not for Livery dinners. On 13 November 1995 the Company withdrew its planning application. The property on St Andrew's Hill was again let for commercial use, and subsequent redevelopment resulted in a marked improvement of the Company's finances and has provided a most welcome annual income ever since.

In 1989 the Company had 278 members. The ways by which a man was admitted to membership had altered since the days when the craft was flourishing. Redemption (by which an applicant was introduced by a member and the payment of a fee) was once unusual but had become the most common method as relatively few members were working smiths. The other two methods, known as servitude and patrimony, were once the common ones. Servitude was where a boy who was not the son of a freeman of the Company served an apprenticeship to a master blacksmith and at the end of his term, upon production of his 'proof piece', was eligible to become a freeman. Patrimony was the term that was used for a boy who learned his trade with his freeman father but who was spared the trouble and expense of entering a formal apprenticeship. In modern times, the terms have been interpreted differently. Boys are sometimes apprenticed to their fathers, even if they are not working blacksmiths, and the rules of Patrimony specify that only those born after the father has received the Freedom are admitted automatically once they have reached the age of 21. In earlier centuries, this rule would not have been necessary as an apprentice was forbidden to marry and would not have had legitimate children before he became a freeman.

In 1992 the Court endorsed the decision by the Wardens to admit ladies who were practising blacksmiths to the Freedom. At the Michaelmas Court in 2004 Mrs Zena Sanders, a freeman since 1992 and the daughter of a Past Prime Warden, was admitted as the first Lady Liveryman. Five years later, Michelle Parker, the Senior Tutor of Blacksmithing at Warwickshire College, became the first lady working blacksmith to be admitted to the Livery.

In 1979 the Prime Warden expressed a desire for a function to be arranged which would include the entertainment of Ladies. This began the following year with a lunch and then in 1982 with a dinner at Glaziers' Hall. Nowadays, the number of Ladies at the annual Banquet at the Mansion House is roughly equal to that of the Liverymen. The Prime Warden's Weekend at a place of his choice has become another well-established social occasion, and an annual Carol Service at the Chapel of Charterhouse, followed by a reception, is now held jointly with the Ironmongers Company. Two Prime Wardens have held their weekends in France and on another occasion the 850th anniversary of the death of St Eloy was celebrated by a trip to Limoges. The most unusual gathering was that arranged by the Prime Warden in 1991, when a meeting of the July Court was held at the ancient hall of the (almost defunct) Incorporated Company of Smiths of Newcastle-upon-Tyne, followed by a Blacksmiths' Dinner, then the following day a tour of the city and a Civic Dinner provided by the Mayor. Another memorable event occurred in 2005 when, for the first time in over 250 years, the Company provided and manned a float to support the Lord Mayor's Show, for on this occasion the Lord Mayor was Alderman

David Brewer, a Liveryman and Honorary Member of the Court of the Company, Past Master of the Merchant Taylors, and future Prime Warden of the Worshipful Company of Blacksmiths.

It is not known how it came about that the Newcastle Company shared the Arms of the Worshipful Company of Blacksmiths, but in 1971 the London company readily agreed to a request from the brewers, Ind Coope Ltd for permission to use their coat of arms at the Blacksmiths' Arms Public House, Thornwood Common, between Epping and Harlow (a pub that has since been demolished). At the same time, the Clerk wrote to all other brewers to say that the Court was now agreeable to the use of the coat of arms at other pubs of this name, but that all designs must be approved by the Company.

The Company's treasures seemed incomplete without the silver Blacksmiths' Cup that Christopher Pym, Clerk of the Company, had presented in 1655, but which had been sold in 1785. At the 1976 Banquet at the Mansion House, the Prime Warden announced that the Cup was to be returned to the custody of the Company, thanks to the generosity of the owner, Lady Brabourne. The Cup was valued at £30,000, so the Company had to insure it at £112.50 per annum, and it was normally to reside at the London Museum. A reception was held for Lord and Lady Brabourne and her father, Lord Mountbatten, and replicas of the Cup were offered to members of the Company and presented as gifts to other companies. Eventually, 111 replica cups were sold, and the Company made a tidy profit of £987.

Sponsorship of the Craft

In 1960 the Company formed a Craft Committee, consisting of six working blacksmiths, four Liverymen and a Chairman selected from the Court of Assistants. The Prime Warden expressed the hope that the new body would form a proper working committee which would inspect the work of craftsmen for awards, report to the Wardens, act as it thought fit, and consider ways and means of furthering the efforts of this section of the Company's work. An important step forward in demonstrating the Company's determination to strengthen its links with the modern craft of smithing had been taken.

One of the committee's tasks was to nominate suitably qualified working smiths as judges for the Agricultural and other Shows at which the Company awarded cups and prizes. In the late 1960s and early 1970s these Shows comprised the Royal Agricultural Society (Kenilworth), the Royal Welsh (Builth Wells), the Bath & West and the South (Bath), the Kent (Maidstone), the East of England (Peterborough), the Northampton (which was soon afterwards combined with the East of England), the South of England (Ardingly), and the county shows of Essex, Surrey and Hertfordshire. By the 1980s the Devon County Show (Exeter) and the Great Yorkshire Show (Harrogate) had also attracted sponsorship in the form of awards and prizes from the Company. By 1994 the Company was represented at an impressive geographical spread of shows at Ardingly, Bristol, Brockenhurst, Builth Wells, Dorchester, Edinburgh (Ingliston), Exeter, Harrogate, Ipswich, Malvern, Peterborough, Shepton Mallet, and Stoneleigh (twice).

The Company's long association with the Rural Industries Bureau continued into the 1960s. For example, prizes and books for apprentices were awarded through the Rural Industries Committees of Suffolk and Warwickshire. In 1968 the Bureau merged with the Rural Industries Loan Fund to create the Council for Small Industries in Rural Areas (CoSIRA), which in the following year held an Exhibition of wrought ironwork at The Building Centre, London. In 1988 CoSIRA was merged with The Development Commission to form the Rural Development Commission.

The Company remains listed among the 'Founder' members of the City and Guilds Institute, but the links were weakened in 1961 when it was decided that as only a small number of candidates joined some of the classes, including that for the blacksmiths, the future provision of examinations were not financially viable; the Institute's blacksmiths' examination was absorbed in its Agricultural and Agricultural Engineering Section. The Company's sponsorship of technical education became focused instead on the Herefordshire College of Technology, upon a suggestion in September 1973 by the National Association of Farriers, Blacksmiths, and Agricultural Engineers, an association which had approached the Company to form a liaison back in February 1961. In 1975 the Company agreed to participate with NAFBAE on an apprenticeship scheme or incentive, providing that the organisational work was kept within bounds. The Craft Committee suggested that as the Herefordshire College of Technology had an apprentice blacksmith course the syllabuses could include a special item for wrought ironwork to a detail approved by the Blacksmiths' Company, and that if an apprentice passed successfully in this item his

The Blacksmiths' Arms, Millhouse Green (Yorkshire). From 1971 the Company has allowed brewers to use its arms on their public houses throughout the country. This sign adorns a pub on the edge of the Pennines, close to where the author lived as a boy.

Tonypandy Cup. George Thomas, Viscount Tonypandy, Speaker of the House of Commons, was an Honorary member of the Court of Assistants. In 1998 Past Prime Warden Lt Col. Delwyn D. Dennis, OBE TD donated the Cup to mark the Speaker's association with the Company. The Cup may be presented annually for the making of a single piece of 'Outstanding Technical Merit'. It is one of the Company's most prestigious awards.

final certificate would be so endorsed, or alternatively the Company could issue a corresponding diploma. On 12 November 1975 an agreement was reached just to award a Certificate of Merit to the apprentice or student smith who gained the highest marks for blacksmiths' work in the final examination of the five-year course. When the College began to provide for a wider range of students, the Company's sponsorship increased.

In 1992 the Prime Warden wrote in the Company's Newsletter:

When I visited Hereford last year to present the students' awards it was a joy to see so many young men and women reaching a high standard in the knowledge and practice of the art and craft of the Blacksmith. It is the intention of the Company that we should make every effort to encourage those who choose to be Blacksmiths.

Brian Owen, Liveryman Blacksmith. The son of a village blacksmith in West Wales, Brian Owen has been involved in many prestigious commissions and restorations for national and local institutions both in London and Wales and is the recipient of many awards.

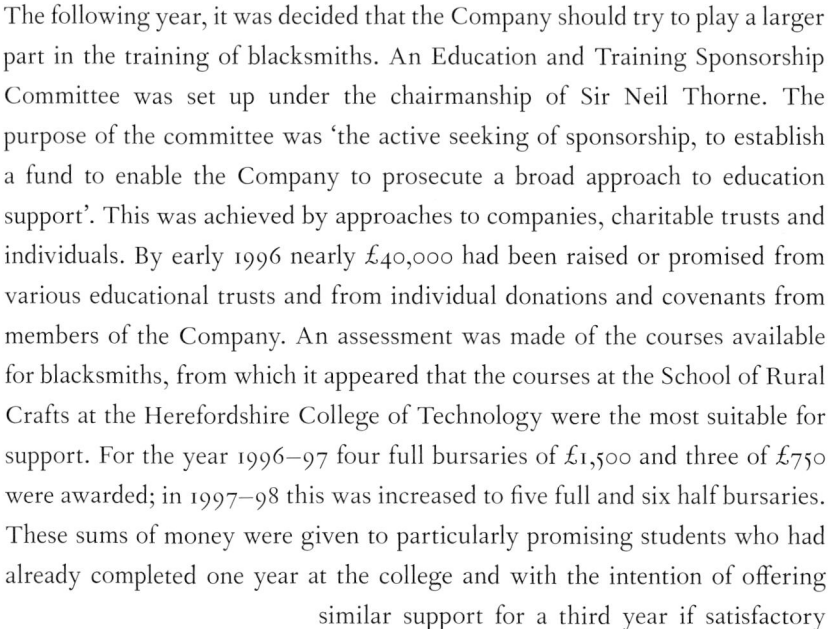

The following year, it was decided that the Company should try to play a larger part in the training of blacksmiths. An Education and Training Sponsorship Committee was set up under the chairmanship of Sir Neil Thorne. The purpose of the committee was 'the active seeking of sponsorship, to establish a fund to enable the Company to prosecute a broad approach to education support'. This was achieved by approaches to companies, charitable trusts and individuals. By early 1996 nearly £40,000 had been raised or promised from various educational trusts and from individual donations and covenants from members of the Company. An assessment was made of the courses available for blacksmiths, from which it appeared that the courses at the School of Rural Crafts at the Herefordshire College of Technology were the most suitable for support. For the year 1996–97 four full bursaries of £1,500 and three of £750 were awarded; in 1997–98 this was increased to five full and six half bursaries. These sums of money were given to particularly promising students who had already completed one year at the college and with the intention of offering similar support for a third year if satisfactory progress was maintained. Some of this money was obtained from educational trusts, but most of it came from the generosity of members of the Livery. The awards scheme of the Blacksmiths' Company has been shown to meet a very real need and has continued to the present day with the award of further bursaries to full-time students of the craft, journeymen, and slightly more experienced smiths. Other valuable support for the Herefordshire College is offered by the Worshipful Company of Farriers and the British Artists Blacksmiths Association.

With the help of such sponsorship, the College is flourishing. In May 2000 the Centre for Rural Crafts, incorporating The National School of Blacksmiths, moved to a new purpose-built unit with 36 forges at Holme Lacy, about

THE MODERN COMPANY

four miles from Hereford. Currently over 300 Farriery and Blacksmithing trainees, recruited nationally, attend each year, making the Centre for Rural Crafts the largest training institution in the country for this area of work. The Blacksmithing and Metalwork courses are based on full-time attendance with the opportunity to progress from the First Diploma to Degree level. The majority of students eventually achieve their ambition of running their own business, designing and making objects in metal, such as gates, railings, and furniture. The Company has also taken an interest in the training carried out at the Somerset College of Agriculture and Horticulture, Cannington, near Bridgewater; the Salisbury Technical College, Wiltshire; Warwickshire College; and the Army Apprentices' College, Chepstow, Gwent. At the Company's Banquet in 1989, the Prime Warden took as his theme the upsurge in activities by the Company and the renewed efforts to encourage the craft by awards and prizes.

This drive to connect with the modern craft of the blacksmith also resulted in partnership with the newly formed British Artists Blacksmiths Association (BABA). This co-operation began in 1979 when Richard Quinnell sent a copy of the Association's first bulletin to the Company's Clerk. BABA's aim was to bring together smiths who were interested in producing only high class and artistic ironwork. The Company decided to subscribe. Three years later, Richard Quinnell asked for closer liaison. In 1990 an exploratory meeting between senior members of the Blacksmiths' Company, BABA, and

The Churchill Screen, St Paul's Cathedral. Erected as a memorial to Sir Winston Churchill in the Crypt of St Paul's Cathedral, the Screen is essentially a series of gates incorporating the armorial devices relevant to his life. It was designed by Silver Medallist James Horrobin and his team at Doverhay Forge. On 30 November 2004, the 130th anniversary of his birth, the Screen was dedicated in a short service attended by HRH The Duke of Kent, Past Prime Ministers, members of the Churchill family and other dignitaries. The Prime Warden represented the Blacksmiths' Company.

Mrs Zena Sanders, the first Lady Liveryman, with Prime Warden John Shreeves at the Painters' Hall on the occasion of her admittance to the Livery at the Michaelmas Court in 2004.

Prime Warden John Smith leads a team of professional blacksmiths, all of them Liverymen, on the Company's Float in the Lord Mayor's Show in 2005. (*From left to right*): Les Armstrong, Clive Mockford, 'Mac' Head (past Master Farrier), Don Barker, Steve Rook and Godfrey South.

the National Association of Farriers, Blacksmiths and Agricultural Engineers (NAFBAE) took place at the Royal Show Ground, Stoneleigh, Warwickshire, when it was agreed that further occasional meetings should be held with a view to exchanging views and combining efforts for the benefit of the Crafts. In 1999 the first Companionship of the Worshipful Company of

Blacksmiths was awarded to Richard Quinnell. His work for his firm of Artist Blacksmiths as designer, craftsman and leader was described as legendary. He was acknowledged as the catalyst for the creation of BABA, which had given blacksmiths, often working in isolation, a new dignity and professional status, and links with fellow craftsmen overseas.

In 1982 the Company made a generous contribution to The Ironbridge Gorge Museum, Shropshire, the birthplace of the modern iron industry, and in June 1989 began a regular series of visits with a weekend there. In 1990 the Prime Warden reported that:

> We have a strong Craft Committee who continue to serve us well in

The Full Court with Prime Warden Keith Gabriel before the Awards Lunch on 16 October 2008 at Stationers' Hall.

upholding a high standard of work. I was very encouraged to find that more than 150 working blacksmiths have received awards and the list continues to grow. We are represented at the major Shows and it is my hope that the Suffolk Show can be added during my year. In recognition of the high standards achieved it is my intention to inaugurate an Awards Dinner at which presentations will be made including that of the National Champion Blacksmith for 1991. This event will be open to all Livery.

Two years later, another Prime Warden spoke proudly of the encouragement that the Company gave to 'the Blacksmiths' Art by encouraging Blacksmiths at all levels of experience to enter various competitions around the country particularly at the County Shows. At the moment we have competitions at approximately ten County Shows where we give cups and plaques'. The Craft Committee appointed blacksmiths as accredited judges for these competitions. The competitors who won prizes at these events accumulated points which went towards an overall award and the title of 'Champion Blacksmith'. The Craft Committee was at the moment compiling a complete list of blacksmiths in the British Isles and was working very hard to promote forge iron work. The Committee also liaised with Colleges and the Army, encouraging instructors to enter for the Company's 'Licentiate Certificate' for teaching the craft. The Company was also heavily involved with the new qualifications for blacksmiths after Britain became more closely involved with the European Economic Community. Determined efforts are being made to justify the Company's continued existence by its generous sponsorship of all that is best in the blacksmiths' craft in many parts of the British countryside.

The Company's top award for prestigious work is a Gold Medal. It was announced in 1998 that for the first time in a number of years the Company had awarded two Gold Medals. The last one had been awarded in 1970, since when procedural difficulties had prevented further awards. The highest award that the company makes, based on technical skills alone, is the Silver Medal. The Gold Medal is reserved to those Blacksmiths who have produced work of a Silver standard over many years and have made a substantial contribution to their craft. The two Gold Medals were awarded to Ron Carter of Trapp Forge, Simonstone near Burnley, where apprentices and blacksmiths were attracted from all over the world, and to Colin ('Tommy') Tucker who set up his own forge at Bexleyheath in 1946, then became the Senior Forgework Officer for fifteen years with CoSIRA, was a founder member of BABA in 1978, and served as a prominent member of the Company's Craft Committee. In 2000 the Company's Gold Medal was presented to Edward Martin, the fourth of his family to operate in a forge established in 1854 at Closeburn, Scotland, Past President of NAFBAE and of the World Farriers Association, a man particularly well known for the many gates that he designed, particularly those made for The Thistle Brewery at Alloa.

From 1999 the Company has also awarded an annual Tonypandy Cup to the blacksmith who produces the best piece of wrought iron work 'of outstanding technical merit' whenever it is judged that a piece is worthy of the award. The Cup was donated by Past Prime Warden Lt Col. Delwyn Dennis in memory of the late Viscount Tonypandy, Speaker of the House of Commons and Honorary Member of the Court of Assistants. The first award was a collective one, commemorated on a plaque at the Globe Theatre, in recognition of the skills of Brian Russell, Richard Quinnell, and 130 blacksmiths worldwide in appreciation of the contribution to the Bankside Gates. The Tonypandy Cup has become the Company's most prestigious annual award.

Sir David Brewer photographed when he was Lord Mayor of London, 2005–06.

A new venture for the Company has been the starting of a good relationship with the cadet movement with support for the Competition in October each year when cadets from all three services compete for the Elworthy trophy. At an Awards Lunch about the same time a huge array of prizes was awarded to 'many very talented blacksmiths'. The Prime Warden spoke of the Company's pride that its awards were now highly recognised and the standards required were very high; as an ancient Livery Company they were lucky to have such a strong traditional craft to support. In 2008 visiting Masters from other companies commented on the atmosphere of support generated by the working smiths for the award winners and the rapturous applause for T. F. M. 'Mac' Head, a Past Master Farrier and an Emeritus Court Member, on his appointment as a Companion of the Worshipful Company of Blacksmiths.

While the Liverymen of the Worshipful Company of Blacksmiths are drawn from a wide range of professions and crafts, the Company has gone

Preparing for the Lord Mayor's Show, 2005. Liverymen Don Barker (foreground) and Steve Rook are both professional blacksmiths and holders of Company medals.

back to its roots and is promoting the craft in ways that its founders, over 700 years ago, would have approved. In 2002 a working blacksmith and Liveryman, Donald Barker, was elected to the Court of Assistants, and in time he is expected to become Prime Warden. The Blacksmiths' Company is unusual among the London livery companies in supporting a craft whose

Masters and Wardens at the Awards Lunch on 11 October 2007 at the Painters' Hall. (*From left to right*) Keith Gabriel (Renter Warden), Alderman Sir Gavyn Arthur (Master Gardener), Peter Rayner (Father), Christopher Rogers (Master Founder), John McCuin (Prime Warden), Mrs Judy McCuin, Rear Admiral David Bawtree (Master Engineer), and John Barber (Third Warden).

skills are still based on those that were practised by its original members. But whereas in the Middle Ages membership of the Company was restricted to those who lived and worked at the blacksmith's craft within the City of London and four miles beyond, nowadays membership extends across Britain. The Company has moved with the times while preserving its proud traditions.

Appendix I

Events attended by the Prime Warden of the Worshipful Company of Blacksmiths, Keith Gabriel, 2008–09

		Date
1	WCB Election Court @ Watermen's Hall	31/07/2008
2	BABA AGM & Forge-In @ Weald & Downland Museum	02/08/2008
3	Worshipful Society of Apothecaries – Installation Dinner	13/08/2008
4	Edenbridge & Oxted Show	25/08/2008
5	"The Army for Today" Reception @ Skinners Hall	02/09/2009
6	RNLI – City Summer Reception @ Little Ship Club	03/09/2008
7	WCB Wardens' Court @ Painters' Hall	04/09/2008
8	Visit to Jubilee Sailing Trust's "TS Tenacious" at Canary Wharf	Ditto
9	Dorset County Show	07/09/2008
10	Gunmakers' Company – Lunch and tour of Proof House	09/09/2008
11	Upholders' Company – Dinner @ Tallow Chandlers' Hall	11/09/2008
12	World Traders' Company – Sheep drive across London Bridge (in support of Lord Mayor's Appeal)	19/09/2008
13	St Paul's Cathedral – Recital & Reception for supporters	23/09/2008
14	WCB Social event: Cruise on *PS Waverley* from Tower Pier	26/09/2008
15	Election of Lord Mayor, Guidhall	29/09/2008
16	Reserve Forces & Cadets Association – Centenary Reception @ HAC	30/09/2008
17	Musicians' Company – Evensong & buffet supper @ St Paul's Cathedral	01/10/2008
18	Butchers' Company – Court & Livery Luncheon	02/10/2008
19	City University – Vice-Chancellor's Address	Ditto
20	Elworthy Sword Competition @ Crowborough Camp (Tri-service event for London Cadets, sponsored by WCB)	05/10/2008
21	Painter-Stainers' Company – Art in City 2008 reception	07/10/2008
22	Security Professionals' Company – Annual Dinner @ Guildhall	Ditto

23	Guild of Freemen – Reception & Beating Retreat @ Guildhall Yard	08/10/2008
24	Fire & Iron Gallery, Leatherhead – HRH Duke of Gloucester's visit	09/10/2008
25	RAF Benevolent Fund – 90th Anniversary Reception @ Imperial War Museum	14/10/2008
26	Construction Livery Group – Awards Ceremony @ Glaziers Hall	15/10/2008
27	WCB Michaelmas Court & Awards Lunch @ Stationers' Hall	16/10/2008
28	REME – Dinner @ Arborfield	Ditto
29	WCB Social event: Trafalgar Night Dinner @ Old Royal Naval Colllege, Greenwich	18/10/2008
30	Army Benevolent Fund – Reception @ Household Cavalry barracks	22/10/2008
31	WCB Awards & Craft Committees	28/10/2008
32	Poppy Appeal Service, St Paul's Cathedral	03/11/2008
33	WCB-BABA Lunch @ Butchers Hall	05/11/2008
34	WCB Finance Committee	Ditto
35	Lord Mayor's Grand Finale Concert @ St Paul's Cathedral	Ditto
36	Silent Ceremony, Guildhall	07/11/2008
37	Lord Mayor's Service of Thanksgiving at West London Synagogue	Ditto
38	Lord Mayor's Show	08/11/2008
39	Clockmakers' Company – Dinner @ Mansion House	11/11/2008
40	WCB Charitable Trust Committee	12/11/2008
41	Imperial Society of the Knights Bachelor – 100th Anniversary service @ St Paul's Cathedral	13/11/2008
42	Lynn Painter-Stainers' Prize 2008 – Private View	17/11/2008
43	Lord Mayor's briefing @ Mansion House	18/11/2008
44	Musicians Benevolent Fund – St Cecilia Festival Service @ Westminster Cathedral	19/11/2008
45	MBF Festival lunch @ Banqueting House, Whitehall	Ditto
46	Cutlers' Company – Court Dinner	Ditto
47	St Paul's Cathedral – Donors' Choral Evensong/Reception	26/11/2008
48	WCB Wardens' Court @ Painters' Hall	27/11/2008
49	Reception for Lord Mayor's 800th Anniversary Awards @ Mansion House	01/12/2008
50	Basketmakers' Company – Court Dinner for Masters & Clerks @ Haberdasher's Hall	03/12/2008
51	City University, London – Awards Evening	04/12/2008
52	WCB Carol Service at St Andrew-by-the-Wardrobe	19/12/2008
53	WCB Epiphany Court @ Painters' Hall	15/01/2009

54	Plumbers' Company – Lunch @ Wax Chandler's Hall	20/01/2009
55	Tin Plate Workers' Company – Inaugural Leslie Chamberlain Memorial Lecture @ City University	21/01/2009
56	Founders' Company – Dinner @ Founders' Hall	26/01/2009
57	WCB Craft Committee	27/01/2009
58	Berry Bros Rudd – wine tasting and lunch	10/02/2009
59	Treloar's School & College – Lord Mayor's Visit	11/02/2009
60	WCB Masters & Clerks Dinner @ Innholders' Hall	17/02/2009
61	WCB Finance Committee	18/02/2009
62	Ironmongers' Company – City Dinner	24/02/2009
63	WCB Wardens' Court @ Painters' Hall	26/02/2009
64	WCB Charitable Trust Committee	10/03/2009
65	REME – Visit to School of Electrical & Mechanical Engineering at Bordon	17/03/2009
66	Chartered Surveyors' Company – Dinner @ Fishmongers' Hall	Ditto
67	Turners' Company – Masters & Clerks Lunch @ Apothecaries' Hall	18/03/2009
68	Mercers' Company – Concert by Yehudi Menuhin students & Supper	Ditto
69	Grocers' Company – Livery & City Dinner	19/03/2009
70	Much Haddam Forge, Hertfordshire – Opening of education room & museum.	20/03/2009
71	Surrey Docks Farm – 'Knives into roses' hands-on forging day for London Cadets	21/03/2009
72	WCB Ladyday Court & Lunch @ Painters' Hall	26/03/2009
73	Lord Mayor's Dinner @ Mansion House	Ditto
74	United Guilds Service @ St Paul's Cathedral & lunch @ Stationers' Hall	27/03/2009
75	Whitechapel Gallery – Lord Mayor's preview	03/04/2009
76	Lunch with Sheriff George Gillon & HM's Judges @ Old Bailey	07/04/2009
	Diana's Tour of Mansion House & lunch @ Cutlers' Hall	09/04/2009
77	Water Conservators' Company – Election Court Lunch @ Cutlers' Hall	16/04/2009
78	WCB Annual Banquet @ Mansion House	17/04/2009
79	Engineers' Company – Installation Common Hall & Dinner @ Painters' Hall	21/04/2009
80	GAPAN Cobham Lecture – Joint Helicopter Command	29/04/2009
81	Shipwrights' Company – Installation Dinner @ Clothworkers' Hall	30/04/2009
82	Goldsmiths' Company – Trial of the Pyx Verdict & Luncheon	01/05/2009
83	North Somerset Show	04/05/2009

EVENTS ATTENDED, 2008–09

84	WCB Awards & Craft Committees and WCB Publicity Committee	05/05/2009
85	Supper with Master Constructor, Roger Adcock @ The City Pipe	Ditto
86	Barbers' Company – Sir Lionel Denny Lecture & Supper	06/05/2009
87	WCB Prime Warden's Weekend – Ross-on-Wye / Hereford	0810/05/2009
88	Sons of the Clergy Service @ St Paul's Cathedral	12/05/2009
89	Tin Plate Workers' Company – Court Dinner @ Stationers' Hall	Ditto
90	Bart's Hospital: Service (in St Bartholomew the Great) & View Day	13/05/2009
91	Painter-Stainers' Company – Dinner @ Mansion House	Ditto
92	WCB Wardens Court @ Painters' Hall	14/05/2009
93	Lord Mayor's Big Curry Lunch @ Guildhall	Ditto
94	City Livery Yacht Club – Cowes Regatta	15-17/05/2009
95	Joiners' & Ceilers' Company – Ladies Banquet @ Vintners' Hall	18/05/2009
96	Visit to HMS Sultan, Gosport	09/01/1900
97	Constructors' Company – Lecture @ City University: Building Quality into Heathrow	Ditto
98	RHS Chelsea Flower Show (invited by M Jacques, FWCB)	20/05/2009
99	WCB Finance Committee	Ditto
100	Old Bailey 100 Concert	Ditto
101	Cutlers in Hallamshire – Cutler's Feast, Sheffield	21/05/2009
102	Visit to Corus & Lunch with Cutlers, Sheffield	22/05/2009
103	Devon County Show	23/05/2009
104	RNLI – City of London III Appeal Finale @ Trinity House	27/05/2009
105	Royal Bath & West Show	30/05/2009
106	Fuellers' Company – Lecture @ Fishmongers' Hall: Richard Budge, Carbon Capture & Storage from Coal	02/06/2009
107	Pewterers' Company – Masters' & Wardens' Dinner	04/06/2009
108	Royal Cornwall Show	06/06/2009
109	Security Professionals' Company – Installation Lunch @ Drapers' Hall	09/06/2009
110	Seafarers UK – Royal Marines Beating Retreat @ Horseguards	Ditto
111	WCB Charitable Trust	10/06/2009
112	South of England Show	11/06/2009
113	Ironbridge City Weekend, Ironbridge Gorge	12–14/06/2009
114	Reserve Forces & Cadets Association – Reception @ Mansion House	16/06/2009

115	Financial Literacy Volunteering Initiative – Reception @ Mansion House	18/06/2009
116	Livery Committee – Dinner @ Barber Surgeons' Hall	Ditto
117	Three Counties Show	21/06/2009
118	Election of Sheriffs @ Guildhall / Lunch @ Butchers' Hall	24/06/2009
119	Lecture & Reception: Plantation of Ulster @ Guildhall	25/06/2009
120	Royal Norfolk Show	01/07/2009
121	Wheelwrights' Company – Lunch @ Pewterers' Hall	02/07/2009
122	Glovers' Company – Awards Lunch @ Drapers' Hall	07/07/2009
123	Innholders' Company – Masters & Clerks Dinner	Ditto
124	Drapers' Company – Annual Service & Lunch	08/07/2009
125	Vote for Sheriffs (contested election)	Ditto
126	WCB Midsummer Court	09/07/2009
127	Royal Show	10/07/2009
128	London Bridge 800th Anniversary Fayre & Sheep Drive	11/07/2009
129	'Not a Master in Sight' Lunch, hosted by WC Basketmakers @ Temple Bar	14/07/2009
130	Great Yorkshire Show	16/07/2009
131	WCB Forge-in @ Rowhurst Forge / Fire & Iron Gallery, Leatherhead	17–19/07/2009
132	Buckingham Palace Garden Party	21/07/2009
133	Royal Welsh Show	22/07/2009
134	Insurers' Company – Dinner @ Armourers' Hall	23/07/2009
135	St Andrew-by-the-Wardrobe – Garden Party	24/07/2009
136	New Forest Show	28/07/2009
137	WCB Election Court @ Merchant Taylors' Hall	30/07/2009

Appendix II

The Masters, First, Upper or Prime Wardens of the Worshipful Company of Blacksmiths

COMPILED BY JACQUELINE A MINCHINTON, HONORARY ARCHIVIST, WORSHIPFUL COMPANY OF BLACKSMITHS

This list of Masters, First, Upper or Prime Wardens is based upon two principal sources. One is the series of Minute Books of the Court, which survive from 1605. In these the terms Master First or Upper Warden are commonly used. Names of Prime Wardens from 1828 (when Moses Kipling, author of the Blacksmith's Song, was Prime Warden), are taken from the current *Directory of the Worshipful Company of Blacksmiths*. The name of William Johnson, Blacksmith, occurs on the 1424 list of the Masters and Founders of the Worshipful Fraternity of St Loy.

1424	William Johnson	
	…	
1605	Mr Hollis	Master
	Mr Bickford	Upper Warden
1607	Mr Bickford	Upper Warden
	…	
1614	P […] Powell	Master
1615	the Choice of wardens for the two years next ensuing	
	Mr Bickeforde	Master or Upper Warden
1617	The choice of wardens for the two years next ensuing	
	[Ralph] Harwood	Master or Upper Warden

(No court book extant for 1618-1625)
Robert Grinkin

1626	Mr Lasher	
	elected on death of Robert Grinkin late Upper Warden	
1631	Mr Wine	
1632	Mr Winn	
1633	Mr Skelte	Upper
1634	Mr Perry	
1635	Mr Perry	
1636	Mr Wyn	
1637	William Shawe	Upper
1638	Mr Perry	
1639	Josias Devoris	Upper
1640	Mr Win	
1641	Nicholas Murren	
1642	Mr Hayward	
1643	Mr Hudson	
1644	Mr Devoris	
1645	Mr Kilborne	
1646	Mr Chaplin	

1647	Mr Murran			1718	Joseph Chamberlin	
1648	Humphry Drake			1719	Joseph Harrod	Upper
1649	John Bromesgrave			1720	Joseph Harrod	Upper
1650	Thomas Laiton			1721	Daniel Quartermain	
1651	Mr Wale			1722	Josiah Insley	Upper
1652	Mr Williamson			1723	Joseph Perrin	Upper
1653	Mr Tasker			1724	John Whicheloe	Upper
1654	Mr Broxon			1725	John Whichelo	
1655	Mr Bull			1726	Deputy John Snart	
1656	Mr Arnold			1727	Major John Snart	Upper
1657	Mr Tasker			1728	Mr Gare	
1658	Mr Shatboult			1729	Thomas Martin	
1659	Mr Locke	Upper		1730	Thomas Martin	Upper
1660	Mr Swift	Upper		1731	John Neale	Upper
1661	Mr Kirkeman	Upper		1732	Adam Dutton	Upper
(No court book extant for 1662–1685)				1733	Edmond Merryweather	Upper
1686	William Hanmer			1734	Thomas Spencer	Upper
1687	[…] Parbery	Upper		1735	John Devall	Upper
1688	Mr Parbery	Upper		1736	Roger Pearson	Upper
1689	Mr Pound			1737	Thomas Winspear	Upper
1690	Mr Tindall			1738	John Blakey	Upper
1691	Mr Cole			1739	John Blakey	Upper
1692	Mr Lee			1740	John Hamilton	Upper
1693	Mr Webster			1741	Robert Medlay	Upper
1694	Mr Tew			1742	Joshua Russell	Upper
1695	Mr Briscoe			1743	Joshua Russell	Upper
1696	Thomas Day	Upper		1744	William Sumner	Upper
1697	Robert Blackett	Upper		1745	John Medlay	Upper
1698	Robert Blackett			1746	William Cooke	Upper
1699	Mr Markham			1747	Robert Medlay	Upper
1700	Thomas Lee			1748	James Green	Upper
1701	Thomas Phillips			1749	Mr Winspeare	Upper
1702	Thomas Phillips	Upper		1750	Samuel Freeman	1st or Upper Warden
1703	Robert Blackett	Upper		1751	John Turner	Upper
1704	Daniel Eames			1752	John Daniel	Upper
1705	Richard Platt			1753	Robert Medley	Upper
1706	Miles Arnold			1754	Thomas Hales	1st or Upper Warden
1707	William Smith			1755	Samuel Robinson	First or Upper Warden
1708	David Wilford	Upper		1756	John Killingworth	Upper
1709	John Harris	Upper		1757	Daniel Thompson	Upper
1710	Thomas Bostall	Upper		1758	George Gilbert	Upper
1711	Mr Waite	Upper		1759	Thomas Hunter of Black Friars	First or Upper
1712	John Searle	Upper		1760	William Hornby	First or Upper
1713	Edward White	Upper				
1714	William Greene					
1715	Thomas Smith					
1717	Robert Hoe	Upper				

Year	Name	Role
1761	Edward Rooke	First or Upper
1762	Thomas Day	Upper
1763	John Hopley	Upper
1764	Jonathan Ely	Upper
1765	John Franklin	First or Upper
1766	John Franklin	Upper
1767	Samuel Read	Upper
1768	William Cook of Hoxton	Upper
1769	Robert Leadbetter	Upper
1770	Edward Upchurch	Upper
1771	John Earle	Upper
1772	William Stockley	Upper
1773	Lewis Powell	Upper
1774	Henry Jones	declined office
	James Phillips	Upper
1775	Peter Lyon	Upper
1776	John Lind	Upper
1777	Francis Meryweather	Upper
1778	William Cooke	Upper
1779	John Horton Esq	Master & Upper
1780	Thomas Russell	Upper
1781	Isaac Colnett	Upper
1782	Arthur Betley	Upper
1783	Gilbert Howard	Upper
1784	Gilbert Howard	Upper
1785	Edward Rogers	Upper
1786	Samuel Whitford	Upper
1787	Thomas Hunter	Upper
1788	John Dowley	Upper
1789	William Dawson	Upper
1790	Thomas Charles	Upper
1791	Thomas Draper	Upper
1792	William Horton	Upper
1793	Robert Le Blond	Upper
1794	Thomas Wilcox	Upper
1795	Daniel Fearon	Upper
1796	Francis Walton	Upper
1797	Isaac King	Upper
1798	William Peele	Upper
1799	Thomas Whitaker	Upper
1800	Reverend Thomas Waters	Prime
1801	Thomas Palmer	Prime
1802	Mr Coles	Prime
1803	Mr Wood	Prime
1804	Mr Hadley	Prime
1805	Mr Cowley	Prime
1806	Mr Wood	Prime
1807	Mr Hale	Prime
1808	Mr Sparrow	Prime
1809	Mr Davis	Prime
	(chosen 6 July 1809; dead by 26 July)	
1809	Mr Sparkhall	Prime
1811	Mr Williams	Master or 1st
1812	Mr Garrett	1st
1813	Mr Rankin	1st Warden
1814	Mr Young	1st Warden
1815	Mr Reeves	First Warden
1816	Mr Green	Prime Warden
1817	Mr Choppin	1st Warden
1818	Mr Roberts	1st
1819	Mr Goode	1st Warden
1820	Mr Dawson	1st Warden
1821	Mr Phillips	1st Warden
1822	Mr Yeomans	
1823	Mr Overton	
1824	Mr Russell	
1825	Mr Hummell	
21826	Mr Whitford	
1827	Mr Evans	
1828	Moses Kipling	Prime
1829	Mr T. H. Wilcox	First
1830	Isaac Wilcox	
1831	Joseph Duckham	Prime
1832	Joseph Wright	Prime
1833	William Ravenhill	Prime
1834	William White	Prime
1835	James White	Prime
1836	Richard Vandome	
1837	John Young	
1838	William Smith	
1839	William Garrett	
1840	Thomas Nias	
1841	William Young	
1842	William C. Goode	
1843	Thomas Gunn	
1844	Henrey G. Horton	
1845	James Farrett	
1846	Nathaniel Hadley	
1847	Samuel Gunn	

1848	Robert Wood	1895	Tom Freer Spreckley
1849	J. Yeomans	1896	F. Bessant Williams
1850	Joseph Wright	1897	John Conquest
1851	John Watt	1898	Rev Alfred Marshall
1852	Joseph Dempsey	1899	John Conquest
1853	George Scammell	1900	Andrew Field
1854	George Scammell	1901	Thomas J. Poulter JP
1855	Rev. Dr Randel J. Waters	1902	Philip Baylis
1856	John Finlay	1903	Arthur L. Poulter
1857	Robert Davison	1904	Thomas E. Watson
1858	Thomas Medwin	1905	Henry Carman
1859	Capt. William Robertson	1906	Alfred Barrow JP
1860	Benjamin Rider	1907	Japheth Tickle (Deputy)
1861	J. G. Dunn	1908	Arthur B. Haxell
1862	Alexander Fraser	1909	Arthur W. Brackett JP
1863	Alderman James Abbiss	1910	John A. Mack
1864	Alderman James Abbiss	1911	Edmund M. Doble
1865	George Wright	1912	John Etherington
1866	Richard Farmer	1913	Richard E. Watt
1867	Charles Ravenhill	1914	David Russell
1868	John G. Hartley	1915	Percival Rees
1869	John G. Nicoll	1916	Edward C. D. Poulter
1870	…	1917	Sir W. H. Harris CMG, ex-Sheriff
1871	John Watt	1918	Sir W. H. Harris CMG, ex-Sheriff
1872	Leslie A. Outhwaite	1919	Col Alfred H. Tubby CB, CMG, MS
1873	William Tozer	1920	William Dommett BA
1874	Thomas Spreckley	1921	George Chillingworth
1875	George R. Firth	1922	Harry F. Purdy
1876	Benjamin Warner	1923	Claud Fraser JP
1877	Robert J. Chillingworth	1924	Arthur W. Elwood
1878	Mark J. Lindsey	1925	Charles Wallington
1879	John Pointer	1926	Sir John Caulcott
1880	William J. Barron	1927	Richard W. Morrison
1881	Thomas R. Huntley	1928	William H. Garrett
1882	John Purdey	1929	Lindesay Poulter
1883	Charles Ravenhill	1930	George H. Robus
1884	Charles Ravenhill	1931	Sir Frederick E. R. Becker JP
1885	John R. Caulcutt	1932	Edward J. Stannard
1886	Ryley T. Ingersoll	1933	Louis S Beale
1887	John Farrand Clarke	1934	Arthur J. Adams
1888	Thomas Poulter	1935	Leonard A. Nicol CBE
1889	Charles W. Demmett	1936	Bertram J. Bowles FRICS
1890	William Williams	1937	Sidney Adams
1891	John D. Link	1938	Sidney Caulcott
1892	John Hayes		
1893	Pearse Morrison (Deputy)		
1894	Robert H. M. Jackman		

MASTERS AND WARDENS

1939	Edwin A. Curtis	1977	James F. Arnold
1940	Percy E. Bowles FRICS	1978	Walter J. Jones MSc.
1941	Mjr F. H. Humphris AAMC, LRCPL	1979	Albert A. Baldwin
1942	Mjr F. H. Humphris AAMC, LRCPL	1980	Eric R. Earey FSVA
1943	Mjr F. H. Humphris AAMC, LRCPL	1981	John Green MA
1944	Hubert E. Shepherd MBE	1982	John C. G. Wegerif CBE
1945	Hubert E. Shepherd MBE	1983	Sir Douglas Bruce-Gardner Bt
1946	A. Willis Stevens	1984	Alfred W. Pennington BSc (Eng.)
1947	Evelyn R. Williams	1985	W/Cdr V. S. W. Smyth DFM
1948	Arthur W. K. Brackett MA, LLB	1986	Peter N. G. Rayner BSc.
1949	Frederick J. N. Brackett FRICS	1987	Gordon A. P. Jewiss T Eng. (CEI)
1950	Frederick J. N. Brackett FRICS	1988	Ralph Gabriel MA, CEng.
1951	George E. K. Blythe	1989	Dr Raymond G. List Litt.D.
1952	Frederick W. C. Barker	1990	Geoffrey W. Hughes
1953	Capt. Alan O. R. Beale MBE, MC, JP	1991	Brian F. Land
1954	Rev. Herbert Payne MA	1992	Colin C. Bates FCGI CEng.
1955	Leonard M. Liell JP	1993	Lt Col Delwyn D. Dennis OBE FCIM FRSA
1956	Brian Bowles	1994	Brian J. M. Iles
1957	Thomas A. Stevens	1995	Clifford S. B. Champion
1958	John F. Arnold	1996	Rodney Lyons
1959	CDR (E.) Kenneth G. Cooch	1997	Timothy S. Herring
1960	Robert G. Chillingworth	1998	John M. Latham
1961	James S. Allcard TD	1999	Hugh A. E. Adams
1962	Walter C. Hetherington	2000	Colonel Sir Neil Gordon Thorne OBE, TD, DL
1963	Philip M. Herring MA	2001	Peter R. Allcard
1964	John F. Kayser	2002	Dr E. B. Graham FI Chem. E
1965	Ronald W. Earey	2003	Rodney K. C. Bole BSc. CEng.
1966	Cecil V. Bowles	2004	John W. Shreeves FRICS, FCIOB
1967	F. T. Addy Taylor	2005	John C. Smith MA (Cantab.)
1968	Sir William Robson Brown MP	2006	John L. Barber MRICS. FASI. FGIS
1969	Joseph Diamond	2007	John S. McCuin, BSc., FCA
1970	Norman Iles	2008	Keith R. Gabriel MSc. DIC. CGeol. FGS
1971	Albert Truelove	2009	Alderman Sir David W Brewer CMG, FIL
1972	Nolan D. Moore MM		
1973	Edwin J. Hughes		
1974	Dr Alan J. Beale MD, Dip Bact; FRC Path; FI Biol.		
1975	Henry C. Johnson		
1976	David H. F. Norris		

Appendix III

The Blacksmith's Song

Words by MOSES KIPLING

Music by FRANK ABERNETHY, Mus.Doc., Oxon., F.R.C.O.

Moderato

In the good old-en days when the Gods con-de-scen-ded To vis-it this Earth and en-light-en man-kind, A-mongst those who most us poor mor-tals be-friend-ed Still

With-draw the u-ten-sils pro-duced by our art, And with them the best com-forts of life will re-treat; With-out Knives or Forks we should look migh-ty smart, As with

Still du-ly de-vo-ted to Love and to Beau-ty Each true Son of Vul-can will ev-er be found; For Ve-nus her-self taught our Grand-sire this du-ty, And with

In 1828 Moses Kipling's Blacksmith's Song was first rendered at the George and Vulture tavern off Cornhill, when Kipling was Prime Warden, to music written by his friend Frank Abernethy. The Company approved and adopted the song, which is now sung each year at the Mansion House banquet.

THE BLACKSMITH'S SONG

Vul - can our Pa - tron the fore - most you'll find: When he
un - sha - ven chins we sat gnaw - ing our meat. With -
all her sweet charms she his gal - lan - try crown'd. And

taught us with An - vil and Ham - mer to mould The
- draw but the Axe, and the Saw, and the Plane, Not a
still ev -'ry love - ly young Maid - en will prove To

Plough-share, the Spade, and the Sic - kle to reap, Had we
Ta - ble or Chair would be made for our use; To the
Vul - can's de - scend - ants most yield - ing and kind; For the

paid for such know - ledge a moun - tain of gold, The
mud - hut we should soon be driv - en a gain— The
good Man of *Me - tal*, in mat - ters of love, Has

130 THE WORSHIPFUL COMPANY OF BLACKSMITHS

pur - chase would still to man - kind have been cheap.
best, with - out us, that man's art could pro - duce. } To the
al - ways the high - est re - gard in her mind.

mem-'ry of Vul-can our voi-ces we'll raise, May he and his sons be re-

-vered thro' the land; May they thrive, root and branch, and en-

-joy hap-py days, For by Ham-mer and Hand all arts do stand.

Bibliography

Adams, A., *The History of the Worshipful Company of Blacksmiths London from early times until the year 1785* (Sylvan Press, London, 1951)

Barron, C. M., *London in the Late Middle Ages: Government and People, 1200–1500* (Oxford University Press, 2005)

Barron, C. M. and Wright, L., 'The London Middle English guild certificates of 1388–89', *Nottingham Medieval Studies*, 39 (1995), 108–45

Blair, J. and Ramsay, N. (eds), *English Medieval Industries: Craftsmen, Techniques, Products* (Continuum, 1991)

British History Online, *Calendar of the Early Mayor's Court Rolls*, <www.british-history.ac.uk/>

Campbell, R., *The London Tradesman* (London, 1747)

Chambers, R. W. and Daunt, M. (eds), *A Book of London English, 1384–1425* (Oxford University Press, 1931)

Chartres, J. A., 'Country Trades, Crafts and Professions' in G. E. Mingay (ed.), *The Agrarian History of England and Wales, VI: 1750–1850 (*Cambridge University Press, 1989), 416–65

City of London Livery Companies Commission: Report and Appendix, vol. 3 (1884)

Coote, H. C. and Tyssen, J. R. D., 'Ordinances of Some Secular Guilds in London', *Transactions of the London and Middlesex Archaeological Society*, IV (1871), 32–5

Elmes, J., *A Topographical Dictionary of London and Its Environs* (1831)

Evans, G. E., *The Horse in the Furrow* (Faber, 1960)

Gadd, I. A. and Wallis, P. (eds), *Guilds, Society and Economy in London, 1450–1800* (Oxford University Press, 2002)

Hazlitt, C., *The Livery Companies of the City of London* (Macmillan, 1892)

Kellett, J. R., 'The Breakdown of Gild and Corporate Control over the Handicraft and Retail Trade in London', *Economic History Review*, 10 (1958), 386–94

Ketteridge, C. and Mays, S., *Five Miles from Bunkum* (Eyre-Methuen, 1972)

Moxon, J., *Mechanick Exercises* (London, 1694)

Palliser, D. M. (ed.), *The Cambridge Urban History of Britain, 1. 600–1540* (Cambridge University Press, 2000)

Riley, H. T. (ed.), *Munimenta Gildhallae Londoniensis, Liber Custumarum*, 3 vols (Rolls Series, XII, 1858–62)

Riley, H. T., *Memorials of London and London Life in the XIIIth, XIVth and XVth Centuries* (London, 1868)

Salter, E., 'A Complaint against the Blacksmiths', *Literature and History*, V (1979), 194–215

Sharpe, R. R. (ed.), *Calendar of Letter-Books of the City of London: H* (London Corporation Record Office, 1907)

Thornbury, W., *Old and New London*, vol. 2 (1878)

Unwin, G., *The Gilds and Companies of London* (Cass, 4th edn, 1963)

The Worshipful Company of Blacksmiths, *Customs and Standing Arrangements* (Blacksmiths' Company, London, 1994)

The archives of the Worshipful Company of Blacksmiths are available for consultation at the Manuscripts Section of the Guildhall Library. A catalogue may be consulted on the website <www.history.ac.uk/gh/black.htm>

Index

Abbis, James 89
Abbott, Mrs 44
Adam of Clerkenwell 6
Adams, Mr 68
Agricultural shows 98–101, 103, 107–8, 114
Allen, Paul 53
Andrew of Stibbenheth 6
Apprentices 43–7, 65–7, 71, 80, 91, 106
Arms of the Company frontispiece, 4, 23, 30, 35, 49, 51, 55, 71, 77, 88–90, 92, 102, 107–8
Armstrong, Les 112
Arnold, Cornelius 24
Arrol, Sir William 90
Assistants 30, 35, 37–9, 41–3, 49, 57, 59–60, 66, 68–9, 71, 73-4, 97
Awards Lunch 115

Baker, Sir Benjamin 90
Barber, John 117
Barge banner 61
Barker, Donald 113, 116
Barnes Villas 91, 103
Barrow, Alfred 81
Bartholomew Fair 42–3
Beadle 24, 32, 34, 42–4, 48, 71, 74
Beale, Captain 101
Beardmore, Sir William, Bart 95–6
Bell, Richard 66
Bickford, Mr 38
Blacksmiths' Chest 53, 55
Blacksmiths' craft and trade 5, 14–16, 60–3, 71–80, 107–17
Blacksmiths' Cup 28, 49, 107
Blacksmiths' Hall 17, 20–5, 27–8, 30–2, 39, 41–3, 48–58, 69–70, 73–5, 82–3, 87, 104
Blacksmiths' Song 97, 128–30
Blythe, Dr G.E.K. 104
Brabourne, Lady 28, 107

Brewer, Alderman Sir David vii–ix, 106–7, 115
British Artists Blacksmiths' Association (BABA 110–14)
Bryan, John 102

Cadets 115
Carter, John 66
Carter, Ron 114
Chaplain 102
Charities 82, 84, 88, 110
Charters 7, 24, 31–4, 36, 41–2, 56–7, 68, 70–2, 74, 86
Churchill Screen 111
City and Guilds 101, 103, 108
City of London:
  Lord Mayor's Show/Procession 35, 43, 51, 61, 74, 106, 112, 116
  Mayor and Corporation 1, 6–7, 10, 12, 14, 22, 25, 27, 42, 51, 62, 73, 86
  Mayor's Court 3–4, 6–7, 12, 69
City of London buildings:
  Bartholomew's Hospital 3, 12, 83
  Greyfriars 17–19, 25, 30, 39
  Mansion House 103
  Rainbow Coffee House, Cornhill 73
  St Paul's Cathedral 3, 11, 21, 39, 41, 48, 52, 111
  St Paul's School 71
  The Tun, Cornhill 11
City of London churches:
  All Hallows-by-the-Tower 102
  St Alban, Wood Street 41
  St Andrew 38, 54, 56
  St Andrew-by-the-Wardrobe 104
  St Anne, Blackfriars 40
  St Benet, Gracechurch 10–11

St Giles, Cripplegate 53
St Giles-in-the-Fields 52
St Martin-le-Grand 3, 17
St Mary, Colechurch 17
St Mary Magdalene x, 22, 24–5, 31, 39–40, 52
St Michael, Cornhill 52
St Nicholas, Fleshshambles 11
St Sepulchre Without Newgate 8, 31, 83
St Thomas of Acre 17, 19
City of London livery companies:
  Armourers and Braziers 36, 42, 91–2
  Basketmakers 80
  Butchers 8
  Carpenters 97
  Clockmakers 36, 41, 67, 91–2
  Clothworkers 8
  Cutlers 91–2
  Dyers 80
  Engineers 117
  Farriers 17, 36, 91–2, 110, 115
  Fishmongers 890, 103
  Founders 117
  Gardeners 117
  Glaziers 106
  Goldsmiths 8, 80
  Grocers 51, 103
  Gunsmiths 36, 41
  Innholders 96
  Ironmongers 11, 63, 91–3, 106
  Loriners 8, 17
  Mercers 17
  Merchant Taylors 107
  Painter-Stainers 49, 53, 55, 92
  Pepperers 8
  Shipwrights 80
  Skinners 25
  Spurriers 7–8, 18, 24, 30–2, 37, 43
  Tylers and Blacksmiths 92

132

INDEX

Vintners 36, 91–2
Weavers 80
Woodmongers 36
Clampard, 'Maister' and Alice 24
Clayton, Revd P.B. 'Tubby' 102
Clerk 24, 31–2, 34, 38, 41, 43–4, 49, 59, 70–1, 74–5
Council for Small Industries in Rural Areas (CoSIRA) 108, 115
Court 44, 59, 64, 82, 84, 86–8, 90–3, 97, 104–6, 109, 113, 116
Craft Committee 108–9, 114
Crocherd, John and Alice 23, 28
Crouch, William 66
Currier, 'Mr Warden' 38
Curtis, Edwin Albert 92
Cutlers' Company of Hallamshire 59, 97–8

Dennis, Lt. Col. Delwyn 109, 115
Devoris, Joseph 37

Ellis, Sir William 94, 97–8
Elwood, Arthur William 91, 98, 101–2
Elworthy trophy 115
Exhibitions frontispiece, 89–91, 94

Father 68, 81, 101, 105, 117
Feasts/dinners 18, 27, 30–1, 37, 43, 49–50, 73, 81–2, 91, 93, 102–3, 106–7
Ferour, William 20
Finances 56, 69–70, 74–5, 81–2, 84–5, 87–8, 91–2, 102
Fire of London x, 11, 22, 50, 52, 55, 58, 63
Foreigners 6, 63, 65, 68
Fourth Warden 80–1
Fowler, Sir John 90
Fraternity of St Loy 4, 16–20, 22–3, 25–6, 29–30, 198
Frazer, Alex 68
Freemen/Freedom 9, 26, 37, 43–4, 63, 65, 74–5, 87, 90, 105–6

Gabriel, Keith 113, 117
Godesfast, Roger 12
Goldsmith, Simon 31
Goswell, Richard and Mary 37–8
Grainer, William 34
Griffith, Matthew 39–40
Guildhall 9, 13–14, 17–18, 25, 27, 44, 55, 61, 67, 69, 90–1, 96

Guildhall Warden 67, 80

Hall, John 66
Harding, William 65
Harpwell, Mr Thomas 34
Harris, Roger 38
Harris, Sir Walter Henry 95–6
Hartlowe, Thomas 25
Hadfield, Sir Robert A. 97–8
Head, T.F.M. 'Mac' 112, 115
Herefordshire College of Technology 108–11
Hetherington, Walter Cranmer 92–3
Hobbs, R. 9
Hodges, John 40
Hollis, Mr and Mrs 38, 43–4
Horrobin, James 111
Horton, John 70–1
House Warden 67, 80
Hove Lodge Mansions 85, 91, 102, 113
Humphris, Major F.H. 105

Incorporated Company of Smiths of Newcastle-upon-Tyne 98, 106–7
'Indian Necklace' 105
Inns and Taverns:
  Bell 30
  Black Horse 54
  Boar's Head 30
  Bull's Head, Cheap 30
  Cock in Bishopgate 54
  Cross Keys 30
  Crown and Hoop 31, 55, 84
  Dagger, Friday Street 34
  George, Old Bailey 30, 84–5
  George and Vulture 74
  Green Dragon x, 22, 54
  Horns, Kennington 74
  Hotel Metropole 91
  Paul's Head, Cateaton Street 73
  Plough, Blackwall 81–2
  Pope's Head 54
  Queen's Arms, St Paul's churchyard 74
  Queen's Head 38, 54–5
  Saracen's Head, Aldgate 30
  Ship, Geenwich 81
  Star and Garter, Richmond 91
  Swan 30
  White Lion 54
Iron and steel Institute 94–7, 100, 103

Ironbridge Museum 113
Iles, Norman 36

Jewiss, Gordon A.P. 9
John atte Holte 6
John of Elsingham 3–6
John of Goyppewyco 6
John of Sholane 6
John the Simple 6
Johnson, William 18
Jones, Samuel 38
Journeymen 8–9, 37, 89, 91

Katherine, widow of Walter of Bury 15
Kempe, John 12
Kipling, Moses 128
Kirkman, Francis 38

Lamborn, John 20
Lawrence of Wimbish 6
Lawson, John 34
Lee, Humphrey 38
Liddiard, Mark 66
Liddiard, Richard and Elizabeth 66
Liverymen of the Company 19–20, 31, 37, 42–5, 49, 51, 65, 69, 73–5, 80, 85–7, 91, 93, 102–7, 110, 115
London streets and districts:
  Aldgate 30
  Baynard Castle 21, 38, 54, 104
  Bermondsey 86
  Blackfriars 40, 104
  Cheapside 17, 30
  Christopher Street, Finsbury 85, 91
  Cornhill 4–6, 11, 21, 30, 74
  Cursitor Street 85, 91, 102
  Deptford 86
  Faringdon 6, 40, 54
  Fenchurch Street 11
  Fleet Lane 84–5, 87
  Gracechurch Street 10–11, 30
  Greenwich 86
  Holborn 55
  Lambart Street 10
  Lambeth Hill x, 21–2, 36, 48, 52, 54–5, 58, 73, 75, 82–4
  Lombard Street 11, 30
  Newgate 17, 25, 83–4
  Old Bailey 31, 34, 54–5, 83–5, 87, 91
  Old Fish Street 22, 25, 30, 39–40, 52

Old Jewry 17
Poultry 17
Puddle Dock/Wharf 38, 54–6, 84
Pudding Lane 52
Queen Street, Cheapside 71
Queen Victoria Street 83
Queenhithe x, 21–2, 29, 54
St Andrew's Hill 55, 84–5, 91, 103–5
Shoe Lane 6
Shoreditch 68
Stepney 6
Southwark 42–3, 55
Thames Street 54
Trig Lane x, 21–2
Vintry 36
West Smithfield 32
Westminster 55, 64
Wood Street 6, 41

Marriott, Mr Samuel 73–4
Martin, Edward 115
Masters of the Company 11, 18, 23–4, 31, 34, 38–9, 44
Masterson, Hugh 24
May, John 6
McCuin, John 117
Medals and prizes 89–91, 99–100, 107–8, 114–15
Meymott, Clement 71
Michael of Wimbish 6
Milo le Fevre 6
Mockford, Clive 112
More, Jeffrey 24

National Association of Farriers, Blacksmiths and Agricultural Engineers (NAFBAE) 108–9, 112, 115
Need, S. 71
Nicholas of Tottenham 6
Norman, Widow 44

Ordinances 8–9, 11–14, 17, 42–3, 57
Owen, Brian 110

Parker, Michelle 106
Patrimony 106
Penny, James 66
Phillips, John 66

Pierce, John 49
Pierce, William 38
Pilgrim, James 70
Plage 51–2
Porter 34, 44
Poulter, Thomas frontispiece
Powell, Mr 38
Presteyn, Edward 31–2, 44, 87
Prime Wardens frontispiece, 36, 80, 84, 89, 92–3, 95, 98, 101, 103, 106, 110, 113–22
Properties of the Company 31–2, 34–5, 37–8, 55, 57, 82–5, 84–7, 91–2, 102–3
Puritans and Dissenters 39–41, 59–60
Pym, Christopher 28, 44, 50, 87, 107
Pym, Michael 38, 41

Quarterage 37, 43, 64, 68–9, 71–2
Quest House 50, 53, 55
Quinnell, Richard 111–13, 115

Randle, ADam 12
Ravenhill, Charles 84, 89
Rayner, Peter 117
Redemption 105
Redgate, Roger 25
Renter Warden 67, 70, 80–2
Reeve, Mrs 44
Richard of Chigwell 6
Robert of Sandwich 6
Robertson, Lt Col. 77
Robinson, John 43
Roger of Woodstrate 6
Rogers, Thomas 25
Rook, Steve 112, 116
Royal Commission on the Livery Companies 86–8, 94, 108
Rural Industries Bureau 98–101, 103
Russell, Brian 115

Samuelson, Mr Francis 97
Sanders, Mrs Zena 111
Scammell, George 100
Schneider, M. Eugene 95
Servitude 106
Shaw, Mr 39
Shepherd, Hubert 105
Shreeves, John 111

Smell, Samuel 36
Smart, Ithiell 40
Smith, John 111
Smith, Seth 71
South, Godfrey 112
Spakman, Isabel and John 24
Sparkes, Mrs 44
Spencer, John 20
Starkey, Mr 38
Stephen of Holte 6
Stephens, William 36
Stocks and shares
Stroby, Hugh 7
Summer entertainments 82, 91

Tailor, Sarah 44
Technical education 90, 93–4, 97, 99, 101, 108–10, 114
Third Warden 38, 80
Thorne, Sir Neil 110
Tonypandy Cup 109, 115
Townes, Henry 70
Townsrow, Thomas 49
Tubby, Col. A. 98
Tucker, Colin ('Tommy') 115–15
Turner, Nicholas 60

Ulster plantation 35–6, 70, 92
Uppert Warden 38–9, 42, 57, 67, 70, 80

Walter, John 20, 25
Walton, John 32
Walton, Mr John Spilman 97
Wapshott, George 74
Wardens 11, 13–14, 18, 23–4, 27, 30, 32, 34–9, 41–4, 49, 54–7, 59, 64–9, 71, 73–4, 80–2, 89, 93–8, 106, 108, 117
West, Henry 55
West, Walter 12
Wharton, John 25
White, Roger 35
Wilkinson, Nicholas 43
William of Sholane 6
William of the Forest 6
Wiltshire, Thomas 35
Wire, Mr 68
Wood, George 66
Wood, Mary 66

Yeomanry 19–20, 24, 30, 37, 69–70

See also the list of Masters, Upper Wardens and Prime Wardens given in Appendix II.